Douglas Gresham

STEPSON TO HIS BELOVED MENTOR, C.S.LEWIS

Jack's Life

The Life Story of C. S. Lewis

Foreword by Christopher Mitchell

DIRECTOR OF THE WADE CENTER, WHEATON COLLEGE

BROADMAN & HOLMAN
NASHVILLE, TENNESSEE

*This book is dedicated to Merrie
just for being her, and that means
everything.*

∞

ISBN: 0-8054-3246-9

Published by Broadman & Holman Publishers,
Nashville, Tennessee

CONTENTS

FOREWORD

One of the most persistent misperceptions about the man C. S. Lewis is that for the greater part of his life he lived safely cloistered away from the typical cares and burdens of normal everyday life. The 1994 motion picture *Shadowlands*, for example, portrays Lewis as an Oxford don who occasionally ventures out from the protective college environment to speak about human pain and suffering even though he himself has not really experienced much of either one. According to the movie, it is not until Joy Gresham comes into his life that he is thrust out from underneath the shadows of Oxford's spires into the bright light of real living. Such a portrayal is troubling simply because it is not true. In fact, anyone who knows the facts knows that it is far from the truth.

Now the wonderful thing about this book is that it succeeds in revealing that side of Lewis that typically is not given much attention. More than all previous biographers, Gresham makes clear that the well-known features of Lewis's life—his academic and literary career, his work as a churchman and apologist—took place within the daily context of an exceedingly demanding domestic existence. He gives us a "Lewis of the everyday" without neglecting those other aspects of his life that have until now taken center stage. For the first time, in the pages of this book, Lewis's domestic life takes its proper place. Whether Gresham intended this I don't know. But given his unique relationship to Lewis, I suppose we ought not be surprised that he emphasizes that part of Lewis's life that he knew best. In ways, I suppose he was better acquainted with The Kilns daily routine than anyone else with the exceptions of Lewis's brother Warren, Maureen Moore, the Millers, and Paxford the gardener (The Kilns's hired help), and perhaps his mother, Joy.

That said, I want to address a criticism that I anticipate is certain to be raised against the book. No doubt at points some readers will feel that the author has drawn an overly pious picture of Lewis. But one must remember that our author believes that Lewis was indeed a saint, and a saint of the most real kind: not someone without flaws, but rather one who aspired to overcome those flaws and in fact did so in many cases. "Jack was not perfect," Gresham stated more than fifteen years ago in his book *Lenten Lands*. "He did not always practice what he preached, though he came nearer to doing so than anyone else I have ever met." Speaking of the contradictions evident within Lewis's views of divorce and remarriage, he goes on to observe: "Jack was not immune to the feeling that *his* case was different." Gresham knows well that not all who have looked into the life of Lewis share his estimate of the stature of the man. But then again, they never were, as our author had been, on the receiving end of a decade of truly saintly acts—acts that in fact continue to inform Gresham's life to this very day.

Gresham met C. S. Lewis for the first time in 1953 as an eight-year-old boy. For much of the next ten years of his life Lewis's home, The Kilns, was his home. During that period Gresham was the recipient of a series of loving actions and practical kindnesses from this celebrated Oxford don that often contrasted sharply with so much else in Gresham's life. He was first warmly received into Lewis's home for a fortnight's visit at a time when he and his brother, David, were still processing the effects of their parents' divorce and their transplanting to English soil with all of its challenges and difficult adjustments. Although reaching out to the children was not easy or natural for Lewis, still he unreservedly gave himself to the boys. Three years later, when Gresham found himself faced with the prospect of losing his mother to cancer, it was Lewis who took him and his brother to the hospital, told them the news, and walked through the entire experience with them. A year later this same man, having fallen in love with Gresham's mother, Joy, married her and willingly took up the role of stepfather. Then, three years later Joy died, and Lewis and the boys faced yet another dark night of the soul, and once again Gresham found in Lewis, now his stepfather, a refuge of comfort, nurture, and provision. My point is simply this, that from 1953 to Lewis's death in 1963, no person played as large and as positive a role in the author's life as the subject of this book. Consequently, it would be surprising, even perhaps dishonest, if Gresham had written a biography that was not at the end of the day a tribute to his stepfather.

What Gresham's vantage point has given to us is a wider lens from which to look out upon the landscape of "Jack's life." With all the attention Lewis is bound to attract as a result of the upcoming release of the motion picture *The Lion, the Witch and the Wardrobe*, it is a salutary thing to be reminded that the man never enjoyed the kind of cloistered, protective, and safe academic life often assumed and at times wrongly depicted. And though there will no doubt be some who will disagree with aspects of Gresham's portrait of Lewis, I for one am grateful that the author has taken the time to tell the story of the man he knew in childhood and has since come to understand as an adult.

—Christopher W. Mitchell, director,
The Marion E. Wade Center

PREFACE

There are several good biographies of C. S. Lewis, or "Jack" as he preferred to be called (if you want to know why, then read this book), and so you might wonder why I would want to write yet another one. I have read all the biographies of Jack, and only two of them were written by people who actually knew him. Indeed, most of his biographers never even met him. All of those books are pretty complex analyses of C. S. Lewis the scholar, C. S. Lewis the teacher, or C. S. Lewis the writer. Some of the books are very good, some of them are very bad, and some of them fall somewhere in between.

To two of those books I owe a great debt of gratitude, for when writing a biography, one needs always to check out one's facts to make sure one has them right. The two books I used most were written by old friends of mine whom I have known most of my life. George Sayer who was once a pupil of Jack's. I knew him as a boy and have liked him ever since. His book, *Jack: C. S. Lewis and His Times*, has been one of my reference sources. The second book I used to check facts was *C. S. Lewis: a Biography*, which was written by two old friends: Roger Lancelyn-Green, who alas is no longer with us but has gone on ahead, and Walter Hooper, whom I have known since the summer of 1963 when he spent some weeks visiting at The Kilns. Walter also wrote the incomparable *C. S. Lewis: A Companion and Guide*, which also was very useful to me.

However, what none of these books, the good, the bad, and the ugly, actually does is merely to tell the story of Jack's life—and he led a pretty amazing one at that. Even if you have never read anything by Jack and know nothing about him, I hope that your reaction to the story of his life still will be "Wow, that's amazing." Jack did lead an amazing life, so I thought it was high time that somebody wrote the kind of biography of Jack that I really would like to read. Nobody has, so I did it myself. This book is my attempt to tell the story of his life, the way it was and the way it happened.

Jack once told me that the two worst kinds of books to write were autobiographies and biographies and that man's worst biographer is always himself because he always judges himself by his own standards and is too gentle with him-self. Jack was harder on himself than anybody I ever knew, and I think he taught me to be at least honest with myself in my own autobiography that I wrote some years ago, my first book, and honest with him in this biography, my second book. You judge for yourself.

Blessings,
Douglas Gresham

INTRODUCTION

A while ago a good friend of mine, Keith Getty, and I decided to write a musical show as a tribute to my stepfather, C. S. Lewis (Jack), for his centenary in 1998. Keith wrote the music, and I wrote the song lyrics and the narrative script. The show was a great success, and this work is partly the result of Keith, and others, insisting that the script was potentially the basis of a book and that I should get stuck in and write it. So here it is.

I have been told, "You can't write a biography of a man like C. S. Lewis without quoting him." So here is the obligatory quote, and it's about writing. Jack told me, "First be sure that you know exactly what you want to say. Then be sure you have said exactly that."

I have tried to follow that dictum as I have written this book. This is not a scholarly work filled with academic analysis or conjecture as to what Jack thought and why he thought it or what he wrote and why he wrote it. This is merely the simple recounting of the story of what I believe to be the extraordinary life of an extraordinary man. I hope that it shows how the power of the Holy Spirit of God flows through our lives and, if we allow it to, makes us far more than we could ever be by ourselves. Jack was the finest man and best Christian I have ever known. I loved him and dearly cherish his memory.

Chapter One

EARLY DAYS AND WORMS

If you are about eight years old, then you are the same age I was when I first met the man who wrote the Chronicles of Narnia. If you are eighteen, then you are the age I was when he died; and if you are sixty, then you are about the same age as I am now. But whatever age you are, if you are someone who reads, then the chances are that you have read something by C. S. Lewis; and if you haven't, then you have a great feast of reading yet before you. His real name was Clive Staples Lewis, but that wasn't his fault, and he certainly didn't deserve it. When he was a small boy, he didn't like the name and soon changed it to "Jacksie" by simply refusing to answer to anything else. It was actually because of a small dog that he was fond of that he picked the name Jacksie, which was what the dog was called. It was run over (probably by a horse and cart as there were almost no cars in the time and place where he was a child), and Jack, as he later became known, just took the name for himself.

When I first met him in 1953, he was already a middle-aged man, already quite famous, and already had written lots of books, including several of the Narnian ones;

2

but just like you and me, he started out as a little child. He wasn't an ordinary little boy, though, because from his earliest years, he was very bright and very imaginative.

Jack was born in a place called Strandtown, which is a suburb of the city of Belfast in Northern Ireland. If you want to find it on the map, it is in the northeastern part of Belfast. In those days, more than a hundred years ago back in 1898, there were no washing machines or electrical appliances, or even electricity in the homes, so Jack's mother Flora and his father Albert had to have several servants to help run the household. It wasn't that they were rich; Albert was what we would call a prosecuting attorney, or DA. It was just that in those days servants were employed to do by hand all the work that in today's world would be done mostly by the housewife or her husband with the help of modern machines.

Shortly after Jack was born, the Lewis household consisted of his parents, Albert and Flora, their eldest son Warren, whom Jack always called "Warnie," and five servants—a cook, a housemaid, a gardener, a nursemaid, and a governess. The nursemaid's name was Lizzie, and Jack loved her dearly. The governess was a lady whose job was to begin the two boys' education, and at first she would have had little to do with Jack but would have been teaching Warnie (already three, he was born in 1895). She taught all the things that children today learn in kindergarten and the first grades of school. The other servants looked after all the things that made a home: lighting the fires (in the kitchen stove for cooking, under the laundry "copper" for washing laundry, and in the fireplaces for heating in winter), cooking, cleaning and laundry, and all the things we normally expect a good mother and housewife to do all by herself. Remember though, that in those days it all had to be done by hand. If you have ever tried to wash bedsheets by hand, you'll have some idea of what it all meant.

The food that Cook prepared was different from much of what we expect to see on the dinner table today, and I suspect that for the most part it was healthier. They didn't know as much about the science of nutrition as we do today, but they knew enough to ensure that meals were well balanced and nutritious. Most important, foods had to be fresh orwell preserved, as there was no refrigeration. The milkman, who brought milk, fresh butter, cream, eggs, and a variety of cheeses to the house, would call every day, as also would the butcher and the baker; and often a vegetable man called a "greengrocer" would call several times a week as well. The fishmonger was also a regular visitor, and houses all had a back door for these people to deliver their wares. It was called the "tradesman's entrance" and usually led directly to the kitchen.

Jack was a happy baby and, for a while, a happy little boy. Belfast in those days was an unhealthy city. The life expectancy of most babies was only about nine years because lots of the illnesses which since then we have almost completely done away with were common, and many of them were quite dangerous. Measles, mumps, chicken pox, diphtheria, whooping cough, and lots of others were serious and often fatal. Diseases like cholera, scarlet fever, and typhoid also were quite common and dangerous. So Jack's parents were careful about taking care of their two sons. They didn't have antibiotics or any of our modern medicines, so even a cold was worrying, and Jack seemed to catch every bug that went around. It seems that he was under attack all the time and yet defended as well. For this reason he was kept indoors, away from the cold and wet of the Irish climate as much as his parents could manage. As soon as he learned to read, he began to spend many hours reading all the books that filled their house. Both Albert and Flora loved to read (no radio or TV, remember) so there were hundreds of books all over the house, and Jack and Warnie soon developed a love of reading.

In Ireland in the summer, it gets light about four-thirty or five o'clock in the morning and often doesn't get dark until almost eleven at night, so the days are very long. When it was warm and sunny in the long summer days, they did go outside. Jack and Warnie had lots of interesting things to do and games to play. They had chess, draughts (checkers if you are American), a game called halma, a board game of battles and soldiers which seems to have long since disappeared, and probably others as well. When they were a little older, they both had bicycles and would ride around to friends' and relatives' houses; but when they were small, they played with things that children had fun with in those days that we seem to have forgotten all about today—bowling a hoop, for example, or whipping a top. Bowling a hoop is easy and a lot of fun. All you need is a hoop—which is a circle of some material, and in those days iron ones off barrels were easy to come by, though today a plastic one would be easier to get—and a short stick about a foot long. The idea was that you rolled the hoop away and then kept it rolling and steered it with the stick while you ran along beside it. After a while you can get good at it and can take your hoop into all sorts of places without ever touching it with your hands. Sometimes Jack would get so excited chasing his hoop along the dusty roads that he would lose track of where he was going, and if Warnie hadn't been along to look out for him, he would have found himself completely lost.

Whipping a top was easy too. You needed a wooden top and a small whip made of a stick with a piece of cord or a thin strip of leather like a leather bootlace tied to it. You set your top spinning and then kept it going by whipping it with the string. It's harder than it sounds, but you can make your top spin for ages and also make it go all over the place when you get good at it. Jack and Warnie both had fun with hoops and tops. Warnie was interested in trains and ships and things like that and was fascinated with the far-flung British Empire and places like India. They also went fishing occasionally in nearby streams and rivers and went for walks out in the local countryside. Their walks together in these years led to a lifelong love of country rambling; and years later, when they were grownups, they walked all over Ireland, Wales, and England, sometimes with friends, and sometimes just the two brothers alone.

Another fascinating part of the two boys' lives was the animals they came across both in books and in the fields and hedges near their home. Beatrix Potter had published a series of books about animals—Peter Rabbit, Squirrel Nutkin, and all the rest. These same animals often were to be found living out their lives right among the trees and bushes where Jack and Warnie walked. There were frogs and toads in the streams and ponds, rabbits in the fields, and squirrels in the trees; foxes had dens in the banks, and badger's setts were not hard to find in the roots of hedgerows. And of course the countryside abounded with horses because in those days horses and ponies were still the main means of transport for most people. Jack loved to see animals and imagined them as talking characters just as Beatrix Potter had. It was the little book *Squirrel Nutkin* that gave Jack his first experience of the kind of delight that makes you so excited all you can do is shiver and say something like "golly, golly." It never lasts for long, and when it goes away, you feel that somehow you have lost something you wish you could keep. Jack called it joy, and he began to wonder where it came from and what it was.

Most of us take the seasons for granted, but Jack soon learned a real appreciation for the changes as the year went by. In Ireland spring is a dashingly dramatic and beautiful time. The brown-grey, seemingly almost dead trees and bushes suddenly explode into bright luminous green buds and glowing blossoms, and everywhere you look is alive with new leaves. Early in the morning as spring erupts its volcano of light and color, birds all start to sing songs of delight to tell you that summer isn't far away. The summer itself is a kind of brooding sultry heaviness of lush greens and quiet warmth.

There were almost no cars around in the early 1900s, so they didn't have to worry as much as you would have to today about being run over, and horses and carts (and even the few cars that there were) did not go very fast most of the time. When Jack was about eight, he saw the first car of his life. He laughed when he told me about it many years afterward, but at the time he was so frightened by it and the noise it made that he jumped off his bike and hid in the hedge till it was gone.

Jack liked his father when he was little, and he dearly loved his mother. Flora Lewis was an exceptional woman. She had a university degree in mathematics, which was unusual at that time, and was an amateur writer. However, overseeing the household took much of her time, and she did not spend a great deal of it with her sons. This is not to say that she was in any way a bad mother. Whenever Jack was ill or frightened, it was to her that he ran for comfort. Jack was also fond of his nursemaid Lizzie, and she would tell him old Irish folktales and fairy stories of the Daoine Sidhe (pronounced "Deena Shee") and the Tuatha De Danaan (pronounced "Tootha Day Dannun") of ancient

Ireland. (These were the ancient faerie folk of Ireland, eventually conquered and displaced by the Milesians.) Jack listened in awe as she told him tales of the adventures of the faerie folk of long ago.

Jack was already showing signs of being a very unusual boy. He read and understood things that most of us don't read until we are almost grown-up. Being kept in the house whenever the weather was cold or wet, and in Ireland that is quite a lot of the time, Jack and Warnie soon learned to play together and read together; and in addition to being brothers, they soon became best friends. Barring a few minor quarrels and disagreements, this was to last all their lives.

Both boys were by nature creative, and once when Jack was ill, Warnie made him a miniature toy garden on the lid of a biscuit tin and brought it to his bedroom. Warnie had made a fine job of his tiny garden, and Jack was amazed and delighted with it. It gave him (he said later) his first experience of beauty, and the sensation of "joy" that he felt on seeing it was to recur at different times throughout his life for what seemed like many different reasons. The two boys also spent many hours making up their own stories about an imaginary country they called Boxen; it was in two parts called Animaland and India, and they peopled their country with animals who wore clothes and talked. They always had paper, pencils, crayons, and paints, and they used them all the time. I suppose the beginnings of Narnia can be seen in this childhood occupation, which was their way of combating the boredom of hours spent in the house while the soft Irish rain fell slowly and steadily outside.

∞

Jack and Warnie and their family moved from Strandtown to a place called Hillsborough and a house that their father had arranged to have specially built for their home. It was a bigger house than the first one and was full of long dusty corridors and empty attics. Jack and Warnie loved the new house and set about exploring and playing throughout its empty spaces. It is customary in Ireland for many houses to have names, and this new house was called "Little Lea." It still stands to this day on the North Circular Road. It was a house that looked out over Belfast Lough, which is the large Belfast harbour, and the two boys spent hours sitting in a window in the attic watching the ships coming and going to all parts of the world. There was a big shipbuilding industry in Belfast in those days, and the boys' grandfather had been a shipbuilder and engineer, so they were interested in watching, way over in the distance, the great ships being built at Harland and Wolff shipyards across the water. When Jack was about twelve, the ill-fated *Titanic* and her sister ships the *Britannic* and the *Olympic* were under construction at Harland and Wolff, and Jack and Warnie watched their huge hulls slowly take shape over the months as they themselves passed through the lough, for by now they were both at boarding schools away in England and had to go there by ship. However, we are jumping ahead too fast. Warnie had been sent away to school in England, to a place called Wynyard School in the county of Hertfordshire, and for the first time in his life Jack was very much alone and lonely. For comfort he spent more time with his mother, and the two of them grew very close.

The first really big event in Jack's life was a tragedy because for some time his mother had been steadily growing more and more ill. At last the doctor was called and long, earnest consultations took place. In the end the doctors decided that she had cancer, and in those days this was even more serious than it is today. Hospitals and treatments were not available, so when she had to have an operation, it was performed right there in the house. The whole procedure was terrifying for Jack who, in February 1908, when the operation took place, was not yet ten years old. Three doctors and two nurses took part in the operation, and the whole house smelled of ether and disinfectants for weeks afterwards. Flora Lewis seemed to get better for a while and was able to go on holiday to the seaside with Jack in May of that year, but by June she was again forced to take to her bed where she stayed until August. Flora was a devout Christian, and when her husband Albert spoke to her of the goodness of God, during the night of August 21, 1908, she replied, "What have we done for Him?" Two days later on the morning of August 23, Flora died.

Jack was desolate. The day she died he was in bed with a toothache and crying for his mother. He could not understand why she did not come to comfort him. Everything safe and warm and comfortable, everything that Jack relied on, was suddenly gone. His life was bleak and different. Jack's father Albert was not very good at controlling his grief; his suddenly changed personality frightened Jack, and Albert's desperate attempts somehow to fill the gap that the loss of his beloved Flora left in their family only made things worse. To be fair to Albert, it was a tough time for him because his own father had died a little earlier that same year, and his brother Joseph died just ten days after Flora. It must have been terrible for him, and he was probably never again the same man that he had been before his world fell apart around him. It is certainly true that he had no idea of how to cope with the household and his family without his wife, and as a result, Jack was to be sent away to school, joining Warnie at Wynyard.

Now for a ten-year-old boy to be sent across the sea away from his home to a foreign country where everybody speaks with a different accent and thinks along different lines is hard enough for him to bear. In Jack's case it was almost astonishing cruelty even though it was done with the best of intentions. Jack was an artistic and sensitive little boy who loved his home and its gentle surroundings in the Irish countryside. He loved the soft welcoming warmth of his homeland and had never been away from his home or from his parents. The only trips away that he had made had been for holidays, and then only for a week or so and accompanied by his mother. Suddenly he had lost his mother, his father had changed into a strange and very different man, and he was exiled far away across the Irish Sea to England, a country where to him everything was strange and unrecognizable. Jack had always had his nurse and governess and the other family servants around him, and now he had no one except Warnie, but Warnie did his best to look after and comfort Jack.

That first trip across the sea began as a great adventure for Jack, for he found that being at sea was something he could do better than Warnie. Warnie suffered dreadfully from seasickness, while Jack was completely untroubled by the heaving and swaying of the ship. Being very young, Jack at first almost thought that he was somehow doing it wrong because he watched his revered elder brother lying in his bunk apparently deathly ill but all the while reassuring Jack that this was perfectly normal. However, the sheer delight of the sea and the ship soon entranced him, starting a love of such things that was to last all his life. The cries of the seagulls wheeling overhead, the roar of the sea, and the whistling of the wind in the rigging of the ship were all things that ever after he loved and longed for. There is a strange beauty about being at sea in a ship, and to Jack it was delightful.

The adventure continued as the two boys caught the train from Liverpool down to London and then continued to the school. Here however, the dream turned at once into a nightmare. Wynyard School and its headmaster were both well past their "use by" dates. Wynyard had once gained a reasonable reputation, but by the time that Jack and Warnie went there, it had deteriorated into the sort of place that Charles Dickens might have written about. The headmaster was an insane sadist whose chief delight seemed to be flogging the boys for little or no reason. His insane rages were the dominating feature of life at the school. Jack had been hurled from what could be described as a heavenly existence, directly into a pretty good imitation of hell. It is easy for us to look back at what happened to Jack and wonder how his father could have been such a fool, but in those days in Northern Ireland or "Ulster," a "good education" almost invariably involved going away to a boarding school, and preferably one in England. Albert acted with what he thought were his sons' best interests at heart and did what he sincerely believed to be the best thing for his two boys.

Part of the problem was that the school had once been quite good, and it takes a long time for such a reputation to die away, and it was partly that the headmaster's madness was not yet recognized (though it was later and he was certified insane and committed to an asylum).

Warnie, big for his age and a fairly tough individual, had never said much about what he considered at the time to be a normal school experience, and thus Albert had no idea of what he was condemning his small and sensitive younger son to. Still it is hard to understand how he managed to pick what may well have been the worst school in all England; indeed it would be hard to imagine a worse one. The place had one classroom, one "dormatory"—a low-ceilinged attic room—and one washbasin, for all the pupils. One bathroom served all in the house, pupils and staff alike. There were no sports facilities at all, merely a small patch of gravel for a playground.

As time went by, the number of pupils at this almost unbelievably bad school dwindled, until when Warnie left to go to Malvern College, there were only five left, one of whom was Jack. For some unknown reason, Jack was never actually beaten by the mad headmaster, though all the other boys seem to have been flogged mercilessly. Perhaps an angel was taking special care of him despite the worst that men could do. Warnie had to survive four years of this brutal school where he was taught absolutely nothing, and Jack was to be there for a year. In the end, a high court action was brought against the headmaster for his brutality to a pupil, and the school finally collapsed. Warnie had devised a simple way of staying out of trouble. The pupils were made to correctly complete five arithmetic problems, or "sums" as they called them, every morning. Warnie soon discovered that they were only checked infrequently and not thoroughly, so he did his five sums every morning without fail; he just didn't tell anyone that he did the same five sums every single day.

Although the school itself taught Jack nothing at all, his experiences there taught him a great deal. He was taken, along with the rest of the school, to church at St. John's Church Watford, and there he began to hear for the first time the real teachings of Jesus Christ spoken by men who really believed them. Jack began to be aware of the presence of God and the nature of Jesus. But the world would do its best (as it always does) to drive this from his mind and his heart over the next ten years of his life, and he would completely lose his faith. Second, he learned the value of uniting with a group of others to suffer, and in the end to defeat, brutality and violence. In the last days of Wynyard School, all the remaining pupils formed a strong bond and faced the insanity of the headmaster with a united front.

The final collapse of Wynyard School made it necessary for Albert Lewis to find a new school for his younger son. Warnie was already attending Malvern College, but Jack was sent to a school called Campbell College in his hometown of Belfast. After Wynyard, Campbell College was wonderful, though there were things about it that didn't impress Jack. At Campbell, Jack first heard poetry read by a man who both understood and loved it, and he listened, enraptured as this teacher, Mr. McNeill, read the great Matthew Arnold poem "Sohrab and Rustum" to his class. (Strangely, many years later I too had a similar experience when a talented teacher, Mr. D. J. F. Hill, read it aloud to my class when I was about the same age as Jack had been.) This was Jack's first real introduction to the majesty of poetry, though he had already begun to read the works of the major poets. Jack was beginning to show the early signs of turning into the man whose works have become known and loved by untold millions of readers around the world. Jack only attended Campbell College for a few weeks, and thus, though it had the great influence on him of introducing him to the power of poetry, there is little else that we need say about it.

Malvern was, and still is, a town in the English County of Worcestershire (where Worcestershire sauce comes from), and it is built on the sides of the Malvern Hills. It is a pretty place and famous for its Malvern Wells and St. Anne's Well, springs of what are supposed to be health-giving mineral waters. Certainly someone from Belfast would be attracted by a town where the water had a reputation for giving good health because the water supply in Belfast was bad and often the carrier of disease. Malvern town was noted for its healthy air, and many people who were ill or thought to be of weak health used to go to live there in the hope that their health would improve. Albert Lewis had always thought of Jack as a boy with a "weak chest," though what he meant by that is something of a mystery. I suppose Jack caught colds often, and being the younger of Albert's two boys, he was the object of Albert's tendency to worry. Most of us don't realize when we are young that one of a parent's main jobs in life is to worry about their children, and although it can be taken so far that it becomes a nuisance, it is a way by which their love for their children can often be seen. Anyway, Albert decided that Jack should go on to join Warnie at Malvern. He was too young still to attend Malvern College, so Albert sent him to a school called Cherbourg, which was the preparatory school to Malvern College, and close to where Warnie was. I suppose he thought that having an elder brother already at school close by would help Jack settle there and Warnie would be able to look after Jack at least to some extent. So, after only half a term at Campbell College, Jack was sent off to Malvern and Cherbourg. Once again the two boys could travel together, and although they were not at the same school, at least they were to be close to each other. It was at Cherbourg that Jack's formal education really began.

Chapter Two

THE BEGINNING OF

WISDOM

Again Jack and Warnie were to travel to school together, and once more they would set out from Belfast by ship to Liverpool, and once more they would be side by side on the journey. The sea would sparkle in the sun, and the seagulls wheeling and soaring on the wind would call and argue as they flew beside and above the decks. There are strong and unusual smells to do with ships and the sea: strange scents of machinery, oil, and in those days, coal smoke, tar, timber, and fishiness all mixed and mingled. Jack would take deep breaths of the air and smile, as the ferry ship pulled away from Belfast and out into the Irish Sea. Once again the two brothers were adventuring together, Warnie hopelessly seasick and Jack loving the short voyage and feeling just a bit guilty for doing so as his beloved elder brother lay retching and moaning in his berth.

By this time though, Warnie was already beginning to imagine himself to be grown-up and was trying hard to seem even more so, a trap that most young people fall

into at some stage and a silly one too because the more
somebody tries to look grown-up, the more obvious it is
that he or she is still a child. It is not until you stop trying
to be grown-up that you really seem to be so. Warnie liked
to think of himself as a man of the world, and as most of
us do at that age, he thought perhaps too much about his
appearance and his image. Today we would say that he
was trying hard to be cool, never realizing that only those
who don't try at all really are cool. Warnie was turning
into an image-conscious young twerp, and his influence
on Jack was such that Jack started to copy him.

It is a good thing that they didn't actually attend the
same school at this time because Warnie was not setting a
good example for Jack, and at school he was hopeless. He
had developed the idea that the main object of school life
was to avoid anything that could possibly be termed work,
most especially if he didn't like it anyway. He felt that all
school rules were to be broken, teachers were there to be
made fun of, and the whole object of life was to have a
good time and to seem to be cool. This started a pattern
that was to ruin his whole life, a pattern that he never
managed to break out of. Warnie was a bright boy, one of
the nicest people I ever met, and was also potentially athletic. Had he ever decided to take any trouble over anything, he might have done well both at school and then
later in life too. However, he made his choices very young,
perhaps in reaction to his mother's death and being sent
away from the home he loved, and as a result, lived a life
filled with misery and defeat.

He was actually a talented writer, even at school, and
he found out early that if he did English essays for his
schoolmates, English essays being the one thing that he
loved to do, they in turn would do his math and his Greek
and Latin for him. So he started a kind of roster system.
He would do essays, another boy would do math, and yet

another Greek and so on; and they thus supported one another in their schoolwork. The trouble with this was that none of them learned much about anything other than their own preferred subject. Warnie told me a long time later that in science class the only thing he ever learned was that if you fill a beaker with cold water and add a drop or two of sulfuric acid and some sugar, you have a reasonable substitute for lemonade. Warnie became a good writer, writing six or seven books. Had he not suffered from the problems that began in his child-hood, he might have been as prolific as Jack.

Warnie was, in fact, a gentle, charming rebel; deter-minedly lazy, he discovered all sorts of ways to avoid work, broke as many rules as he could get away with, and in general was a thoroughly idle boy. Eventually, he was asked to leave the school, which is a polite way of saying that he was chucked out, expelled.

Meanwhile, Jack was at Cherbourg, and while he tried at first to follow in Warnie's footsteps, his heart just wasn't in it because he actually loved to learn. He did not start his Cherbourg career well, however, and was soon in a fair bit of trouble. He had still a lot of catching up to do after the time utterly wasted at Wynyard and felt that the extra work assigned to him was in some way unfair. It was not a pun-ishment but merely an effort to allow him to catch up, but Jack didn't see it that way.

After the fashion of the time, Cherbourg was another small school, with only seventeen boys, and there were four masters to teach them, so the teacher-to-pupil ratio was exceptionally good. There was also the school matron, who is a sort of in-house medical person or nurse to all the pupils. She was a kind lady who saw at once that Jack was virtually an orphan, and her heart went out to this sensitive and lonely child. Miss Cowie was her name, and she and Jack soon became close, and Jack missed her when she left the school. She had for a short while replaced Jack's lost mother. While she had certainly been good for Jack in some ways, Miss Cowie was also bad for him in others. She was a woman whose religious beliefs or thoughts were confused, and she dabbled with vague Eastern ideas and a variety of strange fads. She was at least partly responsible for Jack losing his faith in God and in Jesus and deciding that the whole business was bunk and didn't concern him.

While at Cherbourg Jack began to realize and show his fascination with literature and words. It is perhaps unfortunate that he came under the influence of both Warnie and a master they called Pogo at the same time. Pogo was a young man obsessed with his own appearance and position, and Jack soon began to imitate these two young men, becoming a snob and paying too much attention to his own appearance, what he was wearing, and how he styled his hair.

Literature saved him from becoming a complete waster. His taste in literature at this time was widespread, and like a starving man reaches for food, he would read almost anything put before him. Soon he found the great myths of the Norsemen and became fascinated by the whole concept of "Northerness." It helped that the copies of books like *Siegfried and the Twilight of the Gods* that he saw were illustrated by such brilliant artists as Arthur Rackham, whose designs are stunningly beautiful and romantic.

All Jack's preferences at this time were affected by his admiration for both Warnie and the silly young schoolmaster Pogo. Much later he was deeply embarrassed by a fad that he went through (one which lasted a long time) for the music of Wagner which, many years afterward, he told me he thought to be so vulgar that he blushed when he heard it. I suppose we all look back in embarrassment at the things we did and said, and the things we liked when we were young, but being young is a stage we all have to go through. The trick is to survive it long enough to grow-up without doing too much damage to ourselves or other people along the way.

Jack was changing quickly during the time that he attended Cherbourg School, and one part of him that developed there was his powerful imagination. The walks he took through fields and forests, at first just for exercise, began to take on a different meaning. Every tree began to be the possible home of a dryad or tree spirit, the waters were habitats for naiads or water sprites, and he began to look at the world with both imagination and romance filling his mind with dreams of stories yet untold. He saw in his mind great heroes doing deeds of honor and daring and conquering those who would work evil. His body was changing too as he inevitably changed from a child into an adolescent; and all the difficulties which that presents came to him as to any other young boy or girl. Jack began to do well at Cherbourg, and in the end he stayed there an extra year in order to study, and sit for, a scholarship exam for Malvern College. It was his bad luck that he was sick with a virus when the time came to sit for the exam, but he got up from his bed and took the exam anyway. He won a second-grade scholarship, a remarkable achievement for someone who was by no means at his best. This meant that his school fees, the money his father would have to pay for him to attend Malvern, would be considerably lower. Albert Lewis was thrilled when Jack began to shine in his academic work. Warnie had been a disappointment to him, so Jack's success was encouraging, and he wrote letters to Jack to tell him so.

For outside entertainment Jack and Warnie used to enjoy trips to what was called "The Hippodrome." This was a sort of light entertainment variety theatre that presented all sorts of theatrical and circus-style performances. Jack's enjoyment of it was spoiled by an accident that he witnessed, which put him off this sort of thing for the rest of his life. The act that went wrong consisted of four men on bicycles, carrying, on poles on their shoulders, a huge bowl-shaped basket in which a pretty girl rode around and around on another bicycle. Something happened that resulted in the young girl going over the top edge of the basket, crashing down onto the stage, and being badly injured. Jack was disturbed by this accident and could never enjoy this sort of performance again. For the rest of his life he was so concerned for the safety of the performers that to watch any acrobatic or risky act always made him anxious.

Warnie had enjoyed his lazy years at Malvern but learned little there. Jack was to learn a great deal in the short time he was to spend there, only one year, but be unhappy. There are always some who just don't fit into the mainstream of any school system; those who are not good at games, and Jack wasn't; those who are interested in things that most of the boys find boring, and Jack was. Jack could not find it in himself to regard football or cricket or any organized sport as of any importance but felt that they were something to be avoided as far as possible. Like anybody else, he found himself envying the popularity of those who excelled at sports, but he could not imagine why people who could barely talk were so admired simply because they could run fast and hit or kick a ball accurately.

Jack also resented the school system of the time that made the junior boys the servants of the senior ones. A lot has been written about Jack's attitudes and what he later said about Malvern, and there are those who think that he greatly exaggerated the things he disliked about the place, and those of us who think he was absolutely right, so we needn't waste too much time on it. Jack was one of those studious, sensitive, and serious boys whom the sports enthusiasts always look down on and call insulting names like "nerd" or whatever, and yet he became probably the highest achiever and the most famous of those who were at that school at that time. It is interesting that the most renowned people are often those who worked hard at school at the serious things and left the popularity to others. Jack was a brave and determined boy, and he stuck to what he liked and braved the consequences. One of the results of this is that he slowly became what the English called a "prig." This is someone who thinks that because his personal likes are those of the academic world, he is somehow superior to, or better than, those who would rather play football than read a good book. Jack realized much later that our differences don't necessarily make us better or worse, only different. Jack spent his year at Malvern outside of those close groups that form in any school, looking in and wondering what all the other boys could possibly find so attractive about games and sports. He found the food at the school bad and boring, the games a silly waste of time, and the other boys utterly banal. He detested what the school called "fagging," which was running errands and acting as a general servant to the senior boys. Cleaning someone's shoes or sweeping out their study seemed to him to be time utterly wasted and a form of slavery, and I agree with him wholeheartedly.

Jack lasted a year and wrote several letters to his father asking permission to leave the school. Albert disregarded the letters until at last Jack threatened to shoot himself, and Albert finally took the matter seriously. It is not surprising that Warnie, a tough, carefree boy who wanted to learn nothing and greatly enjoyed wasting his time, was as happy at Malvern as Jack, who desperately wanted to learn, was miserable. Warnie was never able to understand why Jack was unhappy there, and perhaps few people could. George Sayer, a pupil of Jack's at Oxford years later, a longtime friend, and the author of the best biography of Jack yet written, certainly did not really understand what had so oppressed Jack at Malvern, but he had changed sides and become a schoolmaster himself and indeed for many years was a master and then head of the English department at that very school. It is rare for teachers to know what really goes on at the schools in which they teach and sometimes difficult for them even to believe what they are told about those schools by pupils who have been there.

In any case, Warnie, who was by this time already in training at the famous Royal Military College at Sandhurst, was upset that his younger brother was so unhappy. He wrote to their father and suggested that Jack should go where he had been sent when he had been asked to leave Malvern, to W. T. Kirkpatrick at Great Bookham in the County of Surrey.

William Thompson Kirkpatrick had been a headmaster of Albert's old school, Lurgan College, and was by this time, the historic year of 1914, living in semiretirement but taking private pupils for intensive tuition. It is a significant indicator of his abilities as a teacher that Warnie, a lazy and rebellious boy who had learned almost nothing at Malvern, went to Kirkpatrick for three months in 1913, sat the entrance exam for Sandhurst, managed to come twenty-first out of 201 students, and entered The Royal Military College as a prize cadet in February 1914.

And so Jack came to Great Bookham and to "The Great Knock" as he and Warnie came to call Kirkpatrick. Here at last he met a man who was capable of understanding him and indeed of knowing just what he needed to get his mind working to its best abilities. Teachers today talk of things like "stimulation" and "motivation," but Kirkpatrick was a man who knew just what was required to get the very best from each of his pupils.

Jack's life so far seems to have been full of characters that one might expect to find written about in the pages of a book of stories, and we have yet to meet many more. But of all the people who will walk through the pages of this history, none was more extraordinary than The Great Knock.

W. T. Kirkpatrick was, to start with, a physically impos-ing man. He was tall and thin, and he wore what used to be called "side whiskers," that is to say that his face was almost all covered with hair, grey by the time Jack met him, while his chin was clean shaven. It sounds strange today but was fashionable and accepted in 1914. I am sure you have seen old pictures of people who looked like that. His standard of dress was unusual, too, in that he wore old, shabby clothes all the time except on Sundays when he would put on a suit, though that was also pretty old and scruffy looking. He was a keen gardener, and his hands, which were large and strong, were always grubby with dirt. He did not look like a great scholar and philoso-pher, but then the real ones rarely do. It's the people who want to be thought of as great scholars who go to lots of trouble to try to look the part. The real ones just don't bother.

Kirk, as Jack often referred to him, was a strange man to talk to as well. He was firmly convinced that to use speech for any purpose other than the communication of important information or ideas was a complete waste of breath, and so his conversation was always serious and of considerable weight. He never indulged in idle talk at all, and if you were to say something, you had better have thought it out fairly thoroughly before you spoke. Jack soon found out about this, for on his arrival at Great Bookham railway station, he was met by Kirk himself, and Jack idly remarked that the scenery of Surrey seemed to be wilder than he had imagined it to be. Kirk immediately challenged him, asking exactly what he meant by "wilder" and upon what information he had based his expectations in the first place. Jack was soon forced to admit that he had said something that really had no meaning and that he had no right to hold, much less express, an opinion on the subject at all.

Jack soon grew to understand Kirk and his strange ways and also to admire this odd and slightly frightening man. Kirk was from Northern Ireland too, and his accent was one which Jack had been hearing all of his life, and this itself probably gave him a sense almost of home-coming when he arrived at Great Bookham. Several characters that Jack wrote about in his books many years later were based at least partly on Kirkpatrick. Kirkpatrick's wife also was very much a part of the household, and she fed Jack good traditional fare. Bacon, tomatoes, sausages, kippers, and Irish soda bread were all typical Irish break-fast foods. After years of boarding school food, which is usually indifferent and sometimes downright bad (though I have attended two schools where the food was very good), Jack must have really welcomed the change to good Irish cooking, and I am sure that also contributed to his sense of welcome.

I suppose that from our point of view, the most important thing about Kirk was his amazing, almost magical, gift of teaching. Jack soon found that this man could stretch his mind right to the edges of its ability without ever going too far. He had his own unique teaching methods, and they were adapted to suit the needs of each pupil. Having succeeded with Warnie, who was a lazy though bright boy, he began to do the same with Jack, who was intelligent and not lazy in the least. Under his training, Jack learned Greek, Latin, French, and Italian; and he learned them so well that when working in those languages he found that he was even thinking in them. He also learned a great deal of German but not as well as the other languages. He soon was reading the great classics of literature of those countries in the original languages, and he began to realize that he was gifted with a peculiar, rare, and valuable talent, one which he worked hard to develop fully: Jack never forgot anything he read! Later in life this strange memory of his was to be very useful to him.

Kirkpatrick had no appreciation of poetry but was one of those rare men who could appreciate another's love of something without either sharing or understanding it, and he encouraged Jack in this interest. Kirkpatrick was the man who first (in 1914 when Jack was just sixteen years old) recognized that his new pupil had the potential to become a great writer. He also knew at once that Jack's gifts would make him a difficult boy to teach as he was in danger of becoming bored quickly with things of second-rate quality and things in which he could not see any importance.

As Jack began to become a logical and rational thinker and debater, he was becoming at the same time more and more romantic in his artistic side. These two opposite qualities were to wage a war within him until he managed to put them both in their proper place, realizing that he could be both romantic and logical at the same time. Jack also began to try his hand at serious writing. One thing that was a disadvantage about Kirk was that he was an atheist; he had fallen into the trap of believing that his own intellect, his brain power, was so strong that anything he could not prove simply didn't exist. And so good was he at argument that few could have stood against him in philosophical discussions. He failed to ever admit that there might well be things existent, beyond the power of his own mind to recognize or analyze.

Soon enough, Jack, in his admiration for Kirk and with his own burgeoning intellectual power, fell into the same trap. "If I can't prove it, it can't be so." It wasn't for some years that he realized God cannot be proven because He is above and beyond our abilities to prove or disprove, in fact outside of all of our abilities of thought so that at best we can only perceive His bare shadow. Jack became a self-confessed atheist. That is, he freely admitted that he did not believe in God. Actually he was more an agnostic, someone who isn't really sure whether there is a God or not, rather than an atheist, who actively believes that there is no God. To do that really takes more faith than most of us have in God Himself.

While Jack was at Great Bookham, learning and maturing under the guidance of The Great Knock, and Warnie was training to be a soldier at Sandhurst, boys alittle older had begun dying in France in the war that was to claim the lives of ten million men. In those days young men still thought there was something glorious about war. They forgot about the horrors of blowing people to bits and being blown to bits; they hid their minds from the desperately maimed veterans of earlier wars who begged in the streets of the great cities of Europe. They blinded themselves with warlike songs and music, and volunteered by the thousands to mix their blood with the mud of the fields of France. It isn't that they were stupid; it was just the way they had been brought up. They believed in the concepts of

The Empire, all the while forgetting that it was founded on conquest, the killing of the native peoples until those that were left asked for peace and gave themselves to be ruled by their conquerors. French, Germans, British, and Americans all have the blood of their forerunners staining their souls. Young Germans were flocking to join the Kaiser's armies, and young Britons followed suit to join in the conflict for their king and country. The generals and field marshals seemed to treat the whole business as if it were some great game, a sporting fixture in which both teams played "away." It was the young who died, just as it always is. There is no glory in war, but if you are in one, by the time you find that out, it is too late, and you are already neck deep in the horror. The First World War was a stain on our world's history that has never been equalled, not even by the second one. The world had begun to change even faster than the growing boy that was Jack.

Jack was not interested in politics. At home in Ireland in his father's house, politics had been the main topic of conversation; and because in Northern Ireland one simply did not talk to anyone of differing political opinions than one's own, all Jack had ever heard was endless blather of similar political ideas chewed over again and again. *Boring* is hardly a sufficient word to describe such talk, and Jack soon learned to tune out a conversation as soon as it turned to politics. However, even Jack, safely ensconced as he was in the wilds of the Surrey countryside, soon had to become aware of the horrible things that were beginning to take shape in France.

In those days the main methods of transportation were ships, trains, and draught animals, and in a war draught animals meant horses and mules. The soldiers were of two main classifications, infantry or foot soldiers, who fought on foot and often marched to wherever they were to fight, and cavalry, who were mounted on horses and fought and travelled on their horses.

This whole idea of war was to change quickly as people realized that new guns, the heavy artillery drawn by mules and horses and the newly invented machine guns, would soon thrash cavalry into bloody red rags. So the war soon became a contest between batteries of heavy guns and two armies of foot soldiers. Airplanes began to play a part, and even tanks were invented during this fight, but it was the men on foot with their rifles, bayonets, grenades, mortars (bomb throwers), and machine guns, who fought and died to win or lose. It was not long before boys Jack had known at school began to be gazetted (as it was called) as killed in action.

Jack was sixteen when he first went to Great Bookham to be tutored by The Great Knock, and he was to remain with this remarkable man for two and a half years. He was as happy there as he ever had been in his life. It was a golden time, a time the like of which comes all too seldom and to far too few of us, a time when he was free of all worry and strife. He didn't have to worry about bullies or senior boys bossing him around. He didn't have a whole lot of seemingly senseless rules and regulations to contend with. There was good food and enough of it and a warm comfortable bedroom all to himself. It was as close to heaven as Jack could imagine. There was a pond there, and in winter Jack learned to skate on the ice. He had a pair of skates that clamped onto the thick-soled boots that everyone wore in those days, and many years later Jack and Warnie taught me to skate with those same skates, which I clamped on to an old pair of army boots. Jack loved his time at Great Bookham. However, as all things must, this too was to come to an end.

Chapter Three

DARING, DUTY, AND

DESPAIR

In the holidays before Jack's last term at Malvern College, Jack had come to know a near neighbor of his in Belfast, a boy about three years older than himself, named Arthur Greeves. They became friends because of Jack's good nature and good manners. Arthur was sick and in bed, and his mother thought that a visit from someone might cheer him up. Arthur was thought to have a weak heart (though it turned out later that he didn't at all), and his mother used to spoil him and put him to bed as soon as he felt even the least bit tired or out of sorts. Jack, being the good-natured and well-brought-up boy that he was, went along to Arthur's house to visit the lad who was probably not in the least ill but merely bored silly; and much to Jack's surprise, he found that he was reading a book of Jack's beloved Norse myths. At once they were launched into a deep and lively conversation, and the acorn was planted of a relationship that was to grow into a giant oak tree of a friendship, a friendship that was to last for the rest of Jack's life.

It is interesting to look back on because the two boys were different in so many ways. Jack hated the thought of being ill and loathed having to stay in bed. Arthur on the other hand enjoyed being sick and would take to his bed at the slightest provocation or just not get up at all if he didn't feel like it. I suppose that being the youngest of five children, it might have been his way of ensuring that he got his share (and more) of attention from his busy mother. Jack loved to work, while the mention of the word would almost reduce Arthur to helpless weakness.

The two boys became fast friends. So close were they that when they were a bit older, they discussed the secret things of boyhood, girls and what they felt about them. Arthur was not averse to falling in love with almost every girl he met and would tell Jack all about it. Jack was a little less excitable, but he too had his share of longings, and he told Arthur all about his relationships—some real and some imaginary. With Arthur, Jack shared many of the secrets of his heart. Arthur had a fine taste in literature and was already widely read. After all, he spent a great deal of time in bed before radios were invented to say nothing of television; he never went to any formal school and more or less educated himself at home from books until he was twenty-five years old when he went to an art school.

Arthur began to recommend books for Jack to read, and he had such a wide experience of books that he was able to give Jack some good advice in this matter. Jack read everything Arthur wrote to him about, and Jack in turn advised Arthur on what to read next. In this way they both encouraged each other to forge ahead in reading. Soon though, Jack was reading all the great classics of Europe in their original languages, and he left Arthur far behind in this regard.

While he was at Great Bookham, Jack did not spend all his time reading and studying. He also went for long

walks through the wild countryside and again came face-
to-face with the various animals that haunted the woods
and fields. In England in those days, hedges were used
more than fences to separate fields, and then, as today,
each hedge was like a city for wild birds and animals. All
kinds of English songbirds nested in them, and among
their roots foxes had their earths (which is what a fox's
home is called), badgers their setts, rabbits their burrows,
and throughout them weasels and stoats hunted and fed.
Surrey was also home to huge old trees, oaks, ash trees,
horse chestnuts (or "conker" trees) as well as sweet chestnuts and elms. Squirrels leapt and played in the branches,
and the world was alive with sound and movement.
Surrey was a beautiful place back then, but over the years
since, the towns have slowly spread out and grown larger
and larger, many of them just joining up, swallowing little
villages as they did so. Now it is mostly covered with
houses, towns, and motorways. Jack revelled in his walks,
and in his reading as well. Some of the authors he read
were pretty advanced for someone not yet eighteen, but he
also read books by people like John Buchan, H. Rider
Haggard, Mark Twain, Jules Verne, and other more popular writers; he had long loved the works of E. Nesbit.

While Jack was learning and growing, the war also was
growing, though nobody seemed to be learning much
from it. The news from the front always seemed to be bad
no matter which side you were on, and it always was
bad with more and more young men killing and being
killed. It was impossible for Jack to be unaware of all this,
and yet at the time it seemed distant, as if it were some
strange dream of which he was not a part, at least not yet.
Yet even in Surrey, on a still night if the wind was just

right, he could hear the mutter and grumble of the far distant guns in France.

About this time and with the encouragement of Kirkpatrick, Jack began to take his own writing more seriously. He began to have dreams of one day becoming a great poet and worked hard to try and learn as much about poetry and all forms of writing as he could. One author whom he encountered, by what seemed to be complete chance, was to change his whole life. One day at Great Bookham railway station, which like many stations then, had a bookshop where travelers could buy something to read on their journeys, he found a book called *Phantastes* by a George MacDonald. MacDonald had been a minister in Scotland. He had died in 1905, but he left behind a large number of extraordinary books, and *Phantastes* is one of the most extraordinary. It is a fantasy that mixes all sorts of characters and events and keeps the reader alert and wondering all the way through. Jack read it and said later that he was never the same again. In the years to come, he was to read everything that MacDonald had written, and most of it delighted him.

Warnie had gone off to Sandhurst to become a career soldier. Now it was Jack's turn to decide what he was to do with his life. Obviously he wanted to go to a university (he preferred Oxford) and study literature with the hope of becoming a university teacher and a great poet at best, and a schoolteacher or a linguist at worst. However, World War I was by now in full swing, and Jack would be liable to be called up to join the army if he stayed in England. Kirkpatrick had no doubts at all about Jack's ability to gain success at Oxford, but if he returned to Ireland, he would not have to fight in the war. Jack had to make up his own mind which way to go. In the end Jack decided that he would stay in England and would therefore join the British army. Warnie was by this time already serving as an officer in the Royal Army Service Corps, and it may be that Jack decided to follow his brother's example yet again. It is also likely that Jack regarded it as his duty to fight against what he saw as an evil that needed to be defeated. Jack had read so much about the history of the world's great events that he had a well-developed sense of duty. By this time he was amazingly well read, and his knowledge of literature was far in advance of most young men his age. To enter a college at Oxford University, Jack had to sit for two separate exams.

The first was a scholarship exam in order to win some assistance to enable him to be at a college at all because his father really couldn't afford to support him fully. In December 1916, Jack sat for a scholarship exam in classics, which is the study of ancient history and languages like Latin and Greek. Jack was dismayed by the exam as it was a particularly difficult one, and he was convinced that he had failed. Although his first choice, New College, passed him over, University College awarded him its second of three open scholarships.

The second was an exam to gain entrance to Oxford University called Responsions. Responsions was just a simple exam to ensure that the student was capable of the sort of study that every undergraduate must perform, and most students of a scholarship level would not have had to study for it. For Jack though, this was not the case at all because he knew almost nothing about science and was not interested in it, and his ability in math was almost a negative quantity. So after he did the scholarship exam, it was back to Kirkpatrick to study for Responsions. He also studied Italian at this time, when really, he should have concentrated more on science and math. His idea was that if he failed to achieve a career at Oxford, he might enter the government service in the Foreign Office, and speaking several languages would be an advantage.

At this point in Jack's life, it seems that God took a visible hand in his progress. Jack sat for Responsions, and he failed the exam. He failed it because he could not pass the math part of it. He was allowed to sit for it again, but he failed it for the second time. Despite this double failure, for some unknown reason the people in charge still invited him to join University College Oxford, though if he wanted to remain there, he would have to pass the Responsions exam at some stage; and so his career as a scholar began almost unofficially.

It is hard to imagine anything good coming from something as horrible as a war, but as we shall see, God had His own plans for C. S. Lewis.

And so to Oxford, the City of Dreaming Spires, a wonderful place for a romantic who wanted above all things to immerse himself in classical studies. Oxford in 1917 was a quiet and almost painfully lovely place. There was almost no traffic in the city streets, and the quiet so beloved by those who are dedicated to study seemed to flow in and around the buildings and the halls of its ancient colleges and fill the soul with peace. Horses and carriages were still the most common means of transport, as cars were still for the rich and thus were few and far between, although lorries and delivery vans had begun to appear here and there. Students scurried to and fro wearing their academic gowns, and almost the whole city was given over to study and learning. April, the month in which Jack went up to

Oxford, is a lovely month in England, as it is the month that begins to hint at the first promise of spring.

As spring dances on, the trees that abound in Oxford burst into bud, blossoms are soon to be seen everywhere, and spring flowers splash the walks, parks, and gardens with color. Daffodils, tulips, and narcissus begin to give back the brightness of the watery early sun and early dandelions, daisies, and buttercups just start to show their delight at the warming of the year, preparing for the riot of color they are soon to enjoy. Greeted with the sights, sounds, and smells of Oxford in the springtime promise of a new summer, Jack fell completely in love with the place.

If you go to Oxford today, you will find it choked with cars and buses and trucks. Often (as my son James once remarked) the air is too thick to breathe and too thin to plough. Heavy industry invaded the area of Cowley with car factories and such, and the huge numbers of people who came to work there so swelled the population that the place has never recovered. There is a constant roar of engines and wheels all day long, and it is nothing like the gracious, quiet, and lovely place that it once was. But even so, when you have finally managed to put out of your mind the modern-day desecration of the city, it is still a beautiful place. To Jack in 1917, it was heavenly.

Jack was to enter University College, usually called "Univ," on April 26 for the beginning of the summer term and would start a career that would see him in Oxford for the next thirty-nine years barring a short time when he was a soldier in the army.

Jack now entered a new world. His rooms at Univ. were reasonably large and comfortable. He had a servant, employed by the college and known as a "scout," to look after his housekeeping; and his meals were provided.

Dinner was served in a small hall or lecture room as there were not many students at the college. Most of those who should have been there were off fighting in the war. Other meals were brought to him by the scout. Univ was at that time more like a military base than a college, as a large part of it was being used as a hospital for wounded soldiers. Jack did not start formal studies, though, because he was soon to be enlisted in the Officer's Training Corps at the college and would have no time for classical study. The seriousness of the situation that England was in at this time of World War I can be seen in the fact that there were just twelve undergraduates at Univ and of those only three, including Jack, were freshmen. Almost an entire generation of young men was killed in that terrible conflict.

Jack found the O.T.C. training to be physically demanding and not at all what he was used to or liked, but despite that he enjoyed himself immensely. Jack loved the rivers of Oxford and the trees and fields that still surrounded the town in those days. He reveled in swimming and walking whenever his training duties allowed him time off. He was also just beginning to discover the wonderful libraries that Oxford provides. Like most students with the whole world of wisdom still to discover, Jack loved to sit for late hours of the night and talk about all sorts of things, and he joined a variety of clubs and societies. Soon though, he was moved from the comfort of Univ to a more military environment temporarily established at another college called Keble. Here he met the man who was to be his roommate, a likable young man called Edward (Paddy) Francis Courtenay Moore, who, like Jack, was from Ireland. The two young men were soon fast friends.

He and Paddy had a tiny room, more like a cell than anything else, furnished with two iron beds and little else. They had no sheets and no pillows but slept in their

pajamas under woolen blankets. This was the first time in
his life since Wynyard School that Jack had to rough it, but
with his Wynyard experiences behind him, this was not
really much hardship for him.

Paddy's mother had come to Oxford to be near her
son and to see him as much as possible before he was sent
to France to the trenches. She knew all too well that the
chances of him ever coming back were slim indeed. Thus
there entered into Jack's life a person with whom he was
to be associated for more than thirty years. As we have
seen, Jack had long ago lost his mother and had ever since
been bounced around from place to place, some horrible,
some better, but none except Great Bookham ever
homelike. He was only eighteen years old, his father was
immovable from his Belfast security, and Jack must have
been feeling desperately alone and homesick. In any case
he was pleased to be invited by Paddy to join in with his
family on occasional outings. Paddy's mother, Mrs. Janie
Moore, was about the same age Jack's mother would have
been had she lived and was separated from her husband.
Paddy also had a sister Maureen who was about eleven at
that time. Jack delighted in the easy and cheerful family
atmosphere that he encountered in the company of these
three expatriate Irish folk.

Frequently Jack and Paddy were sent out on exercises and
traveled here and there, sometimes billeted in homes
and sometimes sleeping out beneath the stars. This was
supposed to toughen them up for life in the trenches, but
it was complete silliness, for nothing could prepare anyone for the horror and filth of trench warfare. Soon
enough Jack was commissioned as an officer, a second
lieutenant in the Somerset Light Infantry, and was given a

month's leave before being called to active service. During this leave Jack and Paddy made a pact between them that should one or the other of them die in battle, the survivor (if there was one) would care for the dependents and family of the one who had died. If Jack had died, Paddy would have been committed to looking after Jack's dependent family members who at that time were nonexistent though it might have meant taking care of Albert or Warnie should the need arise. If Paddy were to fall, Jack would be duty bound to take care of both Janie and Maureen. This was an agreement that Jack was to take seriously, in keeping with both his romantic nature and his sense of honor.

To this day no one really knows what was going on in Jack's head concerning the relationship he had developed with Janie Moore. Some people like to believe that he had a love affair with her; others, that he simply allowed her to take the place of a mother in his affections. He must have longed so much for a mother at that time, for he was all too well aware that he was poised, about to plunge into the midst of darkness, death, and destruction, unlikely ever to return. The truth is that nobody knows and probably nobody ever will. Certainly, he loved her as well as the family atmosphere that he had grown accustomed to with Paddy's family and that he had missed so cruelly ever since he was ten years old

Also, when his leave began, he was ill with flu or something of that nature. So instead of going straight home to Ireland and his father's house, he spent the first two weeks of his leave with the Moore family at their home in Bristol. Mrs. Moore nursed him back to health, and only then did he return to Ireland and Little Lea. In his place most young men might well make the same decision, but it was the cause of deep distress to Albert Lewis,

who could not understand why Jack would want to be
anywhere rather than at home with him. Albert had tried
desperately hard to fill the gap left in his sons' lives by the
death of their mother and had—as almost all fathers must
in these circumstances—failed miserably. His attempts to
be a friend and companion to his sons had actually driven
them away from him. Albert was unaware of what his
efforts had cost him and was hurt by what he probably
saw as Jack's betrayal. The two were never close, but any
hope of achieving closeness with his sons died in Albert
when he realized that Jack had wanted to spend time with
Paddy's family instead of with him. It was foolish really,
for all fathers have to learn that their children move on,
leave them behind, and cease to be merely a part of their
parents. Jack at eighteen was perhaps a little early in this,
but that itself was mostly Albert's own doing by projecting
him out into the world by himself when he was but nine
years old. Now, ten years later, reaping what he himself
had sowed, Albert was puzzled and upset. Jack naturally
enough was not prepared to discuss the matter.

When he came back from his month's leave, Jack was sent
to a camp near the coastal town of Plymouth where he
was to take charge of a party of men who were under
training. He had virtually nothing to do all day. Once he
had handed his men over to an instructor, he had no further duties until he took command of them again when
they had finished their day's training and then simply led
them back to the barracks. A little over a month later, he
received orders to report to Southampton to catch a ship
to France and the fighting.

   In those days as today, soldiers about to be sent
into battle were given a few days or in this case a mere

forty-eight hours of leave in which to say their good-byes and tidy up any loose ends of their lives. Jack went to Bristol and Mrs. Moore's house, having first invited his father to come and visit him there and see him before he left for France. His telegram to Albert read in part "Report Southampton Saturday. Can you come Bristol? If so meet at station. Reply Mrs. Moore's house." Albert, who must have been dreading just such a telegram, would not, could not, or simply was unwilling to allow himself to understand that Jack was telling him to come at once to Bristol for what was likely the last chance to see his son alive. He sent back a message that said he didn't understand Jack's telegram. I for one do not believe that, and had Albert made the effort to rush to Bristol, it is conceivable the entire history of Jack's life might have been changed. Jack was as hurt by his failure to do so as Albert had been by Jack's spending two weeks of his previous leave with the Moores, and the rift between them that these two events caused was to last for a long time and in fact was never properly healed.

The First World War was different from any other war before or since. Throughout the history of man's fighting himself, soldiers have always journeyed to the battlefield, fought, killed, and died, and then journeyed away again, either to fight again somewhere else or to go home; but World War I was different, horrifyingly different. In this war men journeyed to the battlefield and fought, killed, died, and then stayed. They stayed in the filth, the destruction, the fire, and the blood of the battle; there they lived for days, weeks, months, and even years. Their homes were holes dug into the mire of earth so churned by shelling and bombing for month after month that it was a rancid mess of mixed mud

and blood. The very earth of their world was putrid and rotting. This was the most disgusting and ghastly war of all
man's ferocities. In its blood-soaked madness, ten million
young men died.

So Jack was sent off to war after only four weeks of training. To the hell of fire, explosions, waist-deep blood-
soaked mud, constant shelling, and mortar bomb attacks.
To louse-infested clothes and rat-infested shelters, which
were dug out of the walls of trenches in fields so blasted
by high explosives that nothing living remained in the
churned-up raw soil. There were no trees on the battlefield, no plants, just disease, fire, smoke, mud, blood, the
dead, and those creatures that feed upon them. He arrived
at the front line and took up his duties in the trenches on
his nineteenth birthday, November 29, 1917. He had been
in France only twelve days. It is hard to understand today
just how this could happen: boys, straight out of school,
trained for four weeks, and then thrown into the terrible
tortuous mess of war, but we have to remember that the
mismanagement of this war was such that England and
Germany were both simply running out of men. So many
had been killed so quickly that there just weren't enough
young men left to replace them, so boys were given
the minimum of training and sent off to kill and to die.
Surprisingly (and he was as surprised as anyone was), Jack
was a brave soldier and a good officer. Jack had no illusions about his own knowledge of warfare or about his
training, and he soon learned that his sergeant, a Sergeant
Ayers, knew far more than he ever wanted to learn. This
wise man told Jack things like, "The most dangerous thing

in the army is a lieutenant with a map," and it was he who taught Jack what he needed to know to be a reasonably good officer for the five months of combat that he was to survive. It was also this man whose death saved Jack's life.

Jack fought through months of experiences that he talked about only rarely, and he learned some things he would rather not have known, and others, which left with him a glow that lasted all his life. One of these latter was the fact that no matter what background they came from, there was a kind of loving friendship and comradeship that the shocking and desperate conditions of their lives bred in the men who were compelled to live and die together in this stinking squalor. Jack learned to live in mud, to shave with a razor dipped in a cup of tea shared by half a dozen officers. He learned to eat whatever food was put before him, often within both the sight and smell of dead men, both friend and foe. He learned how to tell the nationality of a dead soldier by the smell of the body as it began to rot. He learned to hurl bombs and bullets at men no older than himself and against whom he held no grudge. He learned to relinquish his humanity and to become a beast of prey.

And all the while, he was writing and reading. It is perhaps surprising, but books were available in the trenches, precious books brought out by officers and men and passed from hand to hand and read again and again until they fell completely to pieces, and a piece of rubber or string was then used to hold the pages together until the mud, blood, and fire finally destroyed them. They were for the most part novels and stories, and also some of the great poets. The soldiers read anything that could and would take their minds far away from the war. The books were read in a sort of desperation to while away the incredibly long and dreary hours of inactivity between the frenzied bouts of savage fighting.

In the trenches Jack worked on a series of poems finally
titled *Spirits in Bondage*, which became his first published
book, appearing in 1918 under the name "Clive Hamilton,"
and also a work of poetry called *Dymer*, which came out in
1926 under his own name. This was the beginning of his
habit of writing wherever he was and no matter what the circumstances of his life. In a sense it was his way of escaping
anything unpleasant that was happening to him. In this way
the war, which finished so much for so many people, also
began many things in Jack's life and a career that may well
have needed the kick-start that only this experience could
have provided.

When I began, as ignorant young men will, to speak
of war and warriors with words of admiration and began
to show that I had some idea that there was something
glorious about it all, Jack told me about a lot of his experiences in World War I. Many of the things that happened
to him, and to thousands of others, were absolutely horrible, like the times when he and his men would advance
across the land between the trenches of the two armies,
"no-man's-land" as they called it, and on the way, some of
the men would become bogged down in waist-deep mud.
Jack and the platoon couldn't stop to pull them out but
had to keep on advancing according to their orders, so
they left the men where they were. After the attack was
over and they were returning to their own trenches, they
would often find these men again, physically unharmed
but completely mindless, as if the horrors of spending a
day trapped in the vile stinking morass and seeing the battle go on all around them while they were unable even
to move simply snapped their minds and reduced them to
nothingness.

Other things were amusing, like the time that he and
his platoon were approaching the shell-destroyed remains
of a French farmhouse. Something made Jack suspicious

of it, so he discussed it with his sergeant, and they decided that the sergeant would take a skirmishing party of men with fixed bayonets around to the back of the house and charge into it, while Jack and the rest of the platoon remained under cover at the front. Jack heard his men go roaring into the house and stood up to see what was happening. As soon as he did, about thirty young German soldiers came running out of the front of the house throwing their rifles away and holding their hands high above their heads. More followed a moment or so later. Jack felt so sorry for these young men who were obviously completely terrified that without really thinking, he walked up to the officers who were leading them and tried to talk to them. It later turned out that these men had heard a rumor that the British were shooting all prisoners. Jack was so excited and tense that he forgot all of his German, and all of any foreign language that he knew except French, and when he addressed them in French, they promptly fell to their knees and began to beg for mercy. It seems that the French actually were shooting prisoners. Jack finally managed to calm them down, and they were getting to their feet to march off as prisoners of war when the sergeant approached Jack and suggested that it might have looked better had he at least drawn his pistol. Jack said that for some reason it had never even crossed his mind. He also learned that there are no atheists in the trenches. When the shells start to fall and explode among them, everybody starts to pray. I learned from Jack and Warnie that no matter what people or newspapers or politicians try to tell you, there is no glory in war.

Jack was soon to be hospitalized with trench fever, a severe flulike illness transmitted by lice, but was returned to the front as soon as he recovered. On April 15, 1918, Jack was ordered to advance his troops behind a barrage of British shells fired by big guns from far behind the lines. The shells were supposed to advance before them and fall and explode ahead of them as they went, the idea being to clear the area into which they advanced of enemy troops. That was the plan, but typical of the mismanagement of that war, something went wrong. Soon the howling shells hurtled over-head began to rain down with deafening explosions. Jack ordered his men over the top of the trench parapet and led them straight toward the enemy as the barrage of high explosives riddled with shrapnel landed ahead of them, blasting the German trenches and soldiers. Then suddenly, as they advanced with bayonets at the ready, the barrage stopped advancing and began to come back toward them. Soon Jack and his men were being bombarded by their own artillery from far behind them, and to his helpless fury Jack watched his men being blown to pieces in the constant roar of their own artillery support. Suddenly Jack saw a blinding light, everything went completely silent, and then the ground came up slowly and hit him in the face. Jack had been hit by both the concussion and shrapnel from a British shell. His trusted sergeant had been between Jack and the shell when it exploded and was blown to bits. Apart from his own efforts to escape, Jack remembered nothing more of the battle.

Chapter Four

THE START OF THE
BEGINNING

Jack knew he was wounded but in a sort of detached dreamlike fashion. Nothing seemed to be real, but he knew that he should try to get back, away from the roar of exploding shells, the thud of impacting bullets, and the screams of wounded and dying men. He began to crawl. He remembered the mud that seemed to build up in front of him as he crawled through the mire of the battlefield and the strange fuzziness of both sight and sound of everything around him. He remembered the relief he felt at being able to rest at last when finally a stretcher party found him. They loaded him onto their stretcher and began to carry him back out of the battle. At last he could stop his desperate efforts to make his body move and could just lie there, relieved of all and any responsibility for anything, even his own safety or survival. A long stretcher ride followed and then a jolting, painful trip by field ambulance back to a hospital in the town of Etaples. It was a day or so before he came out of the shock and was able to find out what had happened to him. He had been lucky as it turned out. He

47

had been hit by shrapnel, the jagged pieces of metal which were designed into the casing of shells in order that they should kill and/or maim as many people as possible when they exploded. Jack had been hit in the chest, the left thigh, and the back of the left hand.

When Warnie heard the news that his younger brother had been wounded and was in the hospital in Etaples, worried sick, he borrowed a bicycle and rode for fifty miles through mud and battle-scarred land to go and see Jack in the hos-pital. For Warnie this was a ride of heroic proportions. He was not an athletic man and indeed was not very fit at all. Warnie's idea of relaxation was a good book and a warm armchair. Nevertheless, driven by the fear that is a partner to love, he made a superb effort and arrived at the hospitalto be kept waiting by the staff until finally he was allowed into the ward to visit Jack. There, somewhat to his annoyance, he found Jack sitting up in bed and very glad to see him. He was greatly relieved but a bit annoyed that he had made his desperate journey for so small a cause, as Jack's wounds were not life-threatening. For some reason all that the hospital had that Jack could keep in his stomach at that time was a large quantity of champagne, and so it became Jack's entire diet for some time. Never again would he willingly drink the stuff. The worst part of the visit for Warnie of course was that having seen his brother and relieved his worries, he then had to ride the fifty miles back to rejoin his own unit.

None of the wounds Jack had suffered was actually dangerous, but they were sufficient to render him unfit for active duty for a long time. Jack was considered to be too ill for treatment in the rough-and-ready conditions of the hospitals in France, and much to his delight, he was sent back to England. He had "stopped a blighty one" as the soldiers called it; in other words, he was wounded badly enough to be sent home.

In May 1918, Jack arrived back in England, sent there to recover from his wounds. He went first to a military hospital in London. Nineteen years old, sick, lonely, and wounded, most of his friends slaughtered in battle, Jack longed for his father to visit him, but once again Albert failed him and would not make the short journey over that same Irish sea across which he had so readily sent the nine-year-old Jack ten years before. I can think of no excuse for this failure. Warnie was still in action, and Jack was lying wounded in the hospital. One would think that Albert would have made any effort necessary to be with his younger son, but he didn't.

Someone who did visit Jack, and often too, was Janie Moore. She had a pretty good idea of what he was going through and did her best to comfort him in his pain and loneliness. At the same time she herself was in need of comfort, for her son Paddy was listed as missing in action. (In September she learned that he had been killed, having acquitted himself nobly in battle.) Mrs. Moore made the effort to visit Jack in London and saw a great deal more of him when, in June, he was considered to be out of danger and was sent to Bristol to convalesce, to regain his strength, and to make a full recovery. While in Bristol, Jack wrote again to his father, pleading with him to come and visit. Again Albert did not.

The piece of shrapnel in Jack's chest was considered to be too close to his heart to be safely removed, so it was left in place, which was not uncommon medical practice in those days, and he carried it with him for the rest of his life.

∞

Janie Moore's son Paddy was gone, buried somewhere in France, and she and her daughter had no one to look after them. Mrs. Moore had been exceptionally kind to Jack, and he had made a solemn promise to Paddy that in the event of Paddy's death in battle, Jack would take Paddy's place in taking care of and protecting both Mrs. Moore and Paddy's sister Maureen, so that's what he did. Jack was even then, at the age of nineteen, a man who believed that his given word was an unbreakable bond. A promise was made to be kept, forever if need be—the same kind of bond that one automatically accepts by the decision to have children, and which Albert his father had broken. Jack moved naturally and smoothly into the place that Paddy had left open when he died in France. Jack called Mrs. Moore "Mother," and she often referred to him as "Boysie."

Throughout his wartime experiences Jack had been writing whenever time allowed. Writing poetry in notebooks, collecting ideas and rhymes, images, and thoughts. In 1918, after he had spent his time convalescing, the London publisher William Heinemann accepted his verses, some of which had been written on the battlefields of The Somme, and published his first book *Spirits in Bondage*. This was a great moment in the young writer's life.

Just a little later Jack was sent from Bristol to yet another military establishment. This time he was sent near the town of Andover in Hampshire, where he was supposed to finish his return to health; and when he was quite fit, he would be sent back to France to continue with the war. Mrs. Moore moved to the town to be near him, and Jack wrote to his father to tell him of her kindness and support.

Once again God seemed to take a hand in Jack's life, and before he was sent back to the fighting, on November 10, 1918, Germany surrendered and the war was over. The relief in the minds of those who still had loved ones in the army cannot be exaggerated, and Jack himself was quietly glad that he would not have to go back and even more glad that Warnie was now safe. Warnie on his part was deeply grateful that Jack had been spared and that he would not return to war.

For many years afterward both Jack and Warnie were plagued by nightmares or at least the same nightmare over and over again—being back in the trenches. It was an experience that never really left them, and countless others were in the same state. Millions more would never dream again, their bodies buried somewhere in the mud of foreign fields.

On December 27, 1918, Albert and Warnie were at Little Lea, and to their surprise, Jack suddenly walked in. The three men celebrated the end of the war and their survival of it, with the first bottle of champagne that Jack ever remembered seeing in that house. Jack felt obliged to drink it, but he did not enjoy it, and he could not celebrate when so many of his friends and acquaintances lay dead somewhere beneath the mud of France. Indeed he found it impossible to understand the joy and celebrations that he saw all around him, for though he was intensely glad the war was over, he could not forget what he had seen and done; and he felt no cause to celebrate with the deaths of so many friends and acquaintances in the forefront of his mind. He felt a deep sense of shame and anger at the terrible waste of all those young lives and was annoyed with those who made merry, seeming to him to have already forgotten the grief and pain of those four years of senseless slaughter. Of his group of five friends from his days at Univ, he was the only one still living.

Once again, at this point, the Holy Spirit of God seemed to have taken control of His wayward son and worked His design for Jack's life. For now at last Jack was able to go back to Oxford and University College to begin in earnest his career as a scholar. The colleges were aware that with so many young men killed in the war, it was going to be difficult to find sufficient students to fill the colleges, or even to half fill them for that matter. And with this in mind, the authorities at Oxford decided that men returning from the war would not have to pass the Responsions Exam, the very exam Jack had already failed twice, and which, with its math section quite beyond him, it is doubtful that he would ever have passed. Under normal circumstances this would have meant that he could never have entered Oxford University and certainly could never have worked there. So if nothing else good ever came out of the First World War (though of course there was much other good that did come of it, but that is a different story), at least it made it possible for C. S. Lewis to study and later work at Oxford.

Oxford after the war was different from what it had been when Jack first went there. There were still few students, only twenty-eight at Univ, but the college and the whole country were setting out to return to normal as fast as possible. Oxford in winter (it was now January 1919) is different from Oxford in summer. It is still beautiful but in a stark, solemn way. The trees, which are so lush in their heavy summer leaves, seem to be asleep, their branches bare and dark. In the early morning, as the sun struggles its way through the mist, the white hoarfrost glitters on the grass, and above the ground fog the towers and spires of the ancient city glow golden as the day awakens. It doesn't really become full daylight till almost nine o'clock and is dark again by half past four in the afternoon.

Jack was always an early riser, and he would be up long before even the roosters considered it time to crow. He would spend hours working as daylight crept over the town. At the other end of the day, he would be reading and working till long after the sky was blackened once again by nightfall.

Jack was happy to be back at Oxford, back at Univ, and able at last to concentrate on his studies. College rules meant that he had to spend his first year living in the college, but Mrs. Moore and Maureen, now that Paddy was dead, were more than ready to accept Jack as the best substitute for a son and a brother they could find and so they moved to Oxford to be near him. When his first year was over, he moved out of the college and set up house with them in their rented home. They were to change their place of living again and again over the next four years, moving from one rented house to another for a wide variety of reasons, but despite this unsettled home life, Jack was at last really able to work. Jack's book *Spirits in Bondage* was published in March 1919, and by the end of April 1920, Jack had won a first-class degree in classical honors moderations, as it was called. In August 1922 he took another first in *literae humaniores*, and in July 1923 he took another first in English.

All this time he was living in constant poverty, trying to eke out his allowance from his father and the benefits of his scholarship to pay not only for his own living expenses and those costs attached to his studies but also in honoring his agreement with Paddy to look after Mrs. Moore and Maureen by paying a lot of their living expenses too. His allowance might well have provided him with a comfortable bachelor life, but it was not sufficient for a family of three. He worked with a dedication rarely to be found either then or today, both at his studies and also at all the everyday chores that make up being the head of a household. He also worked at all the extra tasks that went with taking care of a home, laying carpets, moving furniture, cleaning, and all sorts of domestic duties and jobs. His academic work was constantly interrupted. In 1923, at just twenty-five years old, he was exhausted.

These were difficult years, and although someone whose interests and studies in literature and philosophy might make him an unlikely prospect for admiration, Jack was nothing less than heroic.

Perhaps in some feeling of guilt for his other failings as a father, Albert was extremely generous and kept Jack's allowance going for all this time, despite the fact that several times Jack was inexplicably passed over for jobs that he applied for.

He was finally offered his first paid job at Oxford at his own college Univ in 1924. The job was a year of substituting for a philosophy tutor while the man was away in America. Then at last in 1925 he was elected to a fellowship in English at Magdalen College, to teach both English and philosophy, and he was given a salary and a suite of rooms. His new college address was room 3, on staircase 3, New Buildings, Magdalen College, Oxford. He was to occupy them in comfort and some degree of contentment for almost thirty years until 1954. Much of his finest writing would be done in those quiet rooms, and he taught many students—some of whom became famous men—in the years to follow.

Jack enthusiastically joined a variety of university societies and clubs and was active in debates and discussions. The one scar on his otherwise happy life was his break with his father. Through the hard years of 1920 to 1925, Albert continued to support Jack financially, and Jack may have been embarrassed by his father's generosity and may also have felt guilty about continually taking his money and then spending it in caring for Mrs. Moore and Maureen. For whatever reason, Jack ignored his father and went home to Ireland as seldom as he could, partly perhaps because he understandably preferred the company of his new "family" despite all its difficulties and hardships and also perhaps because he may have found it difficult to forgive Albert for never coming to see him when he was in the hospital, alone, sick, and wounded. Certainly with the expense of taking care of the Moores, he could not afford to travel to Ireland often, and it was not until his new job at Magdalen made him independent that he began to spend more time with his father. In any case, Jack himself was deeply ashamed of ignoring Albert for those years and regretted his behavior for the rest of his life. Jack didn't know it at the time, but Albert had only a short time left to live. In 1927 he began to be in great pain from what was thought to be rheumatism, but in 1929 it was discovered that the real problem was cancer, and he died in September of that year.

This period of time, from Jack's arriving at Oxford after the war to the time of his finally being given a paid position at Magdalen and the death of his father, was one of enormous change in his life. He had gone to war as a boy, nineteen years old, and spent almost half a year living in the most horrific circumstances that have ever been experienced by men. Five months of being shelled, bombed, and shot at, of ordering men to go out and die, of making friends only to see them killed before his eyes a few days or in some cases even hours later. Five months of living in mud, always wet and in the constant stench of blood, fire, high explosive, and the decaying dead. All wars are ghastly, but in all wars both before and since World War I, the battlefield has always been a place where soldiers spent only a short time. World War I was different. In this war the soldiers spent months living, fighting, and dying in the same place, continually being bombed and shelled. If you look at pictures of the mud on those battlefields, completely bare and churned up by all the explosions, and then remember that it was not just a place where the men passed through but their home for months on end, for some even for years, you start to get some idea of what those young men went through.

When Jack was wounded and sent back to England, he was secretly delighted. His sickness, pain, and shock were a small price to pay to get out of the hell in which he had been living. He was suddenly a different person from the callow youth who had gone to war. He had time during his recovery to think about all that he had seen and done, and it left its mark on him. Oxford was heaven in comparison, and it is no wonder that he loved every minute of it. But the war had also taught him the vital importance of making full use of his time and not wasting it, for a returned soldier lives the rest of his life feeling that he may die at any moment, in fact in many cases, almost expecting to, for after time spent in constant danger of imminent death, it's a hard habit to break.

∞

Jack had returned not only to study but also to fulfill his promise to Paddy Moore and to accept the task of looking after Paddy's family. Still only nineteen years old, he was mature enough to shoulder the burdens of taking on a household and family that were his only by default and to work hard to keep them all going. He plunged tirelessly into all that this entailed, the drudgery and housekeeping work such as he had never in all his life had to do, and still he was able to perform brilliantly as a scholar. He didn't shirk the tasks that life had set him; he ploughed into them with energy and determination. Jack was growing up, and fast too. Between the ages of nineteen and twenty-five, Jack changed from a delicate boy into a stalwart man.

When Albert died in 1929, Jack's process of growing-up was complete, and strangely it was he rather than the older Warnie who took Albert's place as the head of the family. Warnie was a captain in the army and was logically the brother who would take over the place that Albert had filled in the Lewis family, but Warnie, as a career soldier, had never had to fend for himself and had already started on a path that was to ruin his entire life. Warnie was already becoming an alcoholic. At this time Warnie drank alcohol for several reasons. One was that it was the fashionable thing to do; all the officers drank, and Warnie was always a man to try to fit in and be popular, and that is always a trap. Another was that Warnie didn't realize, and I suppose that nobody did back then, that alcohol is not a stimulant, something that lifts you up mentally and emotionally, but a depressant, something that crushes down your natural thoughts and emotions, so that your fears and embarrassments are squashed. After drinking alcohol, you tend to do all sorts of things that you probably wouldn't do if you hadn't had any alcohol. Of course when the effect of the drink wears off, you feel terrible about the things you have done, but by then it's too late.

Warnie always felt "better" when he had a few drinks; he wasn't afraid any more, and he didn't feel shy any more. His natural and important feelings were squashed, but then they came back stronger than ever when he was sober. His answer to this was simply to stay just a little bit drunk whenever things were tough. The opposite would have worked even better; staying completely off the drink would have eventually cured him of shyness and fear as he matured, but he didn't know that, and so he began to drink too much.

Jack and his "family" had moved from house to house and place to place, always renting whatever they could afford, always living as cheaply as they could manage and always in what was for them grinding poverty. They were always unsettled and for the most part uncomfortable. England in those days was a tough place in which to be poor, for in the winter it was difficult and expensive just to keep warm.

Every time the family moved, Jack did most of the heavy work of carrying boxes and cases filled with their belongings and heaving furniture from place to place. It is strange how much stuff a family seems to gather around itself in the everyday business of just living. It has been said that junk expands to fill the space available to it, and anybody who has moved a few times will vouch for the truth of that statement. Every time you move, you seem to have more things to move, and it was certainly the case with Jack and the Moores.

I suppose we need to have little things that we call our own just to make us feel that even if we have to move, there will always be some things that we take from house to house. Some things are constant in our lives—things that we will always have with us and will make us feel at home no matter where we go, possessions that we regard as treasures just because we are used to having them around. We won't part with them even though they make moving a difficult and laborious job.

Jack seemed to spend a good part of his life packing, moving, and then unpacking all the household bits and pieces, and yet he still managed to work hard at his job and his writing at the same time. Soon Jack began to long for the family to find a place of their own, somewhere they could afford to buy and to stay without needing to move on again after a few weeks, months, or years. When Albert Lewis died, Warnie and Jack decided to sell Little Lea. Neither of them thought that they would ever want to live there again, and they decided that with the money they made from the sale, they would join with Mrs. Moore and whatever money she could raise, and buy a house, which they would all share. Buying a house, especially the first house one buys, is always a difficult and important job. The house has to be right for you, so you go to great trouble to find the perfect one. For Jack and Warnie it was difficult indeed. They knew that what they would really love was probably beyond their abilityto buy because it would be too expensive, but they set out to search and see what they could find.

Chapter Five

THE KILNS

About eight hundred years ago, Oxford became a city of learning. Colleges were founded, and commissions to build them were given out to architects and builders. Stone was needed, and so men went out looking for suitable places where good building stone could be found. The Cotswold Hills were a good source of good stone, but they were a fair distance from Oxford, and stonecutters looked for somewhere closer as well. They found a good site for stone just at the foot of a hill called Shotover, near the village of Headington, which was just outside the city of Oxford, and on the already well-developed London Road. It is important to have a good road to and from a quarry because the stone has to be moved, in those days on carts, to wherever the buildings are to be built.

Soon a new village of sorts was established. It was called, sensibly enough, Headington Quarry because that was how it started. Most villages in England way back then got their start and their names for practical reasons. Either they were named for the family who owned them or for what they did. Even Oxford itself was named for the fact that it was built up, house by house, at a shallow stony place in the river where oxen could cross by ford-ing, or walking on the bottom of the river, without being swept away or sinking into the mud.

Headington Quarry started off as just that, a quarry site. Great chunks and blocks of stone were cut from the ground and dressed, which means shaped and smoothed, and taken off to Oxford to build college buildings. There was a demand for houses and other buildings in Oxford too, and many of them needed stone. Lots of smaller pieces of stone were left over of course, and soon the workers and their employers used this to build cottages and houses for them-selves. They built as close to the quarry as they could so that they didn't have far to go to get to work.

Soon the village was up and running. The quarry needed iron and steel tools, so a forge was built to make them and a cottage for the blacksmith to live in. Horses were used to haul the blocks of stone and, harnessed into carts, to take the dressed stone down to Oxford; and they needed shoes and shoeing, so the blacksmith attended to that as well. He also made the locks for the sheds and houses and the keys to fit them. I know because when I was a boy of eleven, I worked for one of his descendants at that very forge, pumping the big bellows that blew the coal fire into a fierce flame to heat the steel. Old locks and keys were still piled up in the yard. Bill Stowe was my employer's name, and he told me all the old stories about Headington Quarry and about how his father and grand-father had both been smiths before him.

Quarrying was, and still is, hard, dangerous, and dusty work. At the end of a long hard day, the stonecutters and masons needed somewhere to go to slake their thirst and to spend time in relaxation, so there were soon several pubs in the village. The word *pub* is short for "public house," and that meant a house that the public was welcome to visit to drink ales and ciders. Later, when serving alcoholic drinks became a licensed occupation, they would serve wines and "spirituous liquors" as well.

The first pub in Headington Quarry and the closest to the quarry itself was The Mason's Arms, but The Six Bells and The Chequers were soon to follow, for masons and stonecutters are thirsty men. All three pubs are there to this day. The thriving community needed a place of worship too, and later on Holy Trinity Church, Headington Quarry was built, and a parish school to go with it. All around the village were fields and woods, and a short distance away was the London Road.

The stone from Headington Quarry turned out to be not as good as that from the Cotswold Hills and didn't last more than a couple of centuries in the buildings of Oxford's colleges, and so most of it has long since been replaced in rebuilding and repair work. Building with stone is difficult and takes a lot of skill because the blocks of stone must either all be carefully cut to the same size and shape, which takes a skilled stonecutter and a lot of time, or they must be laid all together different sizes and all, and that takes a very skilled stonemason and is a slow process. Building with stone was soon too expensive, and any new big buildings were beginning to be built of bricks instead. So as stonecutters and masons slowly faded away, becoming scarce and expensive to hire, brick makers and bricklayers became more popular.

The quarry became less and less busy. Slowly the men who worked at the quarry retired and were not replaced, and the business slowly wound down. Those who lived in Headington Quarry found other ways to earn their livings, and the village which had been a bustling, busy place, centered on the quarry, turned into a quiet, sleepy little place where nothing much ever happened.

∞

Bricks are much easier to build with than stone because they are all the same shape and size, and they are lighter and easier to handle. Also, you can make bricks almost any color you want them to be. A short way up the road from Headington Quarry Village, just under the northern side of Shotover Hill, farmers had known for a long time that there was a large area of heavy, pale blue-grey clay, the kind that pottery or bricks can be made of. In the latter part of the 1800s, someone had the good idea of digging this clay out of the ground and making bricks from it. Today most bricks are made by machine, but back then it was all done by hand. First you get hold of wet clay, and then you pack it into a brick-shaped mold. You turn this mold out onto a flat surface to dry; and when it is dry enough, you bake it in a hot furnace. This firing process turns the clay into a hard, almost stonelike waterproof substance. When they are properly fired, the bricks are allowed to cool and then taken out of the furnace and shipped off to wherever they are to be used. There was almost always more than one furnace in any place where bricks were made because you had to have one furnace firing while another was being either loaded or unloaded after the fire was out and the bricks were cool enough to handle. Sometimes different chemicals are added to the clay to change the color or the hardness of the bricks for special purposes. The special furnaces for the firing of bricks are called the kilns.

Up the Green Road from Headington Quarry, there was a good supply of good brick clay, and so some men bought nine acres of land and started to dig it out of the hillside. Soon they found that there was enough to make it worthwhile to build a pair of kilns and a brick drying shed or barn right there beside the hill. The bricks they used to build the kilns were brought from somewhere else and were not very good quality, but soon they were built and the men started to make bricks in them—good bricks, strong and light. The kilns were tall furnaces built to look a bit like upside down flowerpots or old-fashioned basket beehive skeps with chimneys sticking out of them. They were making lots of good bricks before 1900, and quite a few of the men from the village of Headington Quarry began to work at the kilns, so a lane was paved from the kilns down to Green Road so that the bricks could be shipped out. Soon Headington Quarry bricks were being used in Oxford and all over the county for building college buildings, houses, barns, sheds, and all sorts of buildings.

Business was booming, and a manager was appointed to run the kilns, so he needed a house to live in, and it had to be close to the brickworks. So, in about 1920, they took bricks and built him a house. It was a nice house, and when anybody asked him where he lived, he would always say, "At the kilns." The house had its own water supply from a spring high up on the hillside overlooking the house, and the water was clear, cold, and delicious. It was piped down to the house from a small reservoir tank built around the spring, and arrived under great pressure, foaming and spurting out of the taps in the kitchen and bathroom.

The clay on the hillside began to be used up, but that didn't worry the brick men. They just started to dig it out of the ground, and quite soon they had a deep pit—about twenty feet deep in some places—which, quite naturally, filled up with water. They didn't care too much; they just kept digging the clay out through the water, using a steam-powered machine that today we would call a dragline shovel. However, in the end the clay began to run out, being more and more difficult to dig out of the ground. The kilns themselves were old-fashioned, and the business could no longer compete with much more modern and efficient brick factories, so at last the brickworks closed down.

The whole property was sold off and became a private home. Trees and forest plants began to grow on the hillside, and the lake that used to be the clay pit soon had fish and all sorts of grooblies living in it. It was still called The Kilns, and its new owners put a tennis court in front of the brick-drying shed and built a little brick seat beside the lake where you could sit and feed the fish. Gardens were planted, and it became a pretty place, which if given time and care would obviously become quite beautiful. Slowly young trees grew up on the hillside, and soon it became a small woods. The lake gradually grew the plants and the animal species that abound in English waters. Fish came into the lake, probably brought by birds, as fish eggs stick to the feet of wading birds and thus are spread from lake to lake. Soon there were roach, a small silvery fish with orange-colored fins, and perch, similar but with spines along their backs.

The lane leading down to Green Road, called Kiln Lane, was a poor road, badly paved and, by this time, full of potholes and puddles. There was one farmhouse away across Kiln Lane and a cottage down near the lane itself, but other than those, just open fields and the occasional copse of trees. The Kilns soon became a lovely, secluded place, quiet and solitary, and the wood with its lake began to be a place of astonishing beauty, still and peaceful most of the time. A story was told many years later that one of the workmen at the clay pit had come to the pit when drunk one night and had tumbled into the water and drowned and that his ghost was sometimes seen walking disconsolately around the lake. The poet Percy Bysshe Shelley is said to have spent time walking in the wood around the lake, musing on his poems. Whether any of that is true or not, I don't know, but the unusual stillness and quiet of the place does lend it a kind of strange secret atmosphere, and it is easy to think that even if it is not haunted, it should be.

In 1930, the people who lived at The Kilns decided to move, and so they offered The Kilns for sale. In 1930, Jack, Warnie, and Mrs. Moore were hunting for a house to buy—somewhere they could be in their own home, peaceful and quiet, comfortable and suitable for a family and yet surrounded by beauty. They found The Kilns. I think it was God's idea.

Jack and Mrs. Moore were the first to see the place, and they could hardly believe their good fortune. It was exactly what they were looking for; in fact it was so good that it was far better than anything they ever expected to find that they would actually be able to afford. But the lovely little house with its nine acres of grounds, its gardens, the woods with the lake in it, and the flat, tree-covered area right at the top of the woods, was all for sale for thirty-three hundred pounds, and they thought that if they all put in as much as they could afford to, they could raise that amount. The two of them fell completely in love with the place as soon as they saw it, and immediately summoned Warnie, who was at that time stationed at an army base in a place called Bulford, to come and look at it with them to get his opinion.

Warnie journeyed to Headington to spend a week with Mrs. Moore and Jack, and as soon as he arrived, on the afternoon of Saturday, July 28, 1930, they began to tell him all about this wonderful house they had found called The Kilns. They were so enthusiastic that Warnie began to worry that the place could not be anything as good as they made it out to be, but on the morning of the following day, Jack took him to inspect the property. As soon as he saw the place, Warnie was as enthusiastic as any of them, and he and Jack clambered all over the woods and walked all around the place looking at the wonderful gardens, the tennis court, the woods, the lake, and at the house itself (though on that occasion they did not go inside).

Warnie and the rest of the family held a summit meeting and argued back and forth to make sure they ironed out any possible disadvantages of the place before making a decision. (This is an important procedure to go through with any really big decision and especially when buying a house.) Finally they all decided that the only drawback they could see about The Kilns was that it was three miles or so from Magdalen College, and that meant that Jack would have to travel to and fro to fulfill his college duties. Jack did not mind that in the least as for him a three-mile walk was enjoyable exercise. In the end the decision was unanimous; they simply must buy it if they could possibly afford to. This meant that they had to find thirty-three hundred pounds. Warnie could put in eight hundred, Jack managed a thousand, and Mrs. Moore was able to put in fifteen hundred. This added together was the exact purchase price. So Jack and Warnie went to see Jack's good friend Owen Barfield, who had been a student with him at Oxford and was now a lawyer in London, to make sure that everything was done properly. The house was to be bought in Mrs. Moore's name with Jack and Warnie getting the house for their home for the rest of their lives should Mrs. Moore die, and then on their deaths it was to pass to Maureen.

And so The Kilns was bought and paid for, and the family started to make plans to move in and also made plans to build on two extra rooms, to be a study and bedroom for Warnie.

∞

This is how the house was arranged when they first went there.

If you go in through the front door, there was a short hall, with two rooms off it: to the left the sitting room and to the right the dining room. Then a sort of L turn with a corridor leading off to the right to the stairs and the kitchen area. Behind this corridor was a room, which was to become at different times a music room or a staff bedroom.

The sitting room and the dining room were both equipped with fireplaces for warmth in the winter. If you went on down the corridor, you passed the stairs on your left, and then the bathroom and the lavatory also on your left, and then came the kitchen and through it to its left was the scullery. A scullery is a room with deep sinks, and it is there that vegetables from the gardens would be cleaned and made ready for cooking, and the dishes would be washed after meals. Beyond the kitchen was a staff bedroom, which had its own fireplace. (Even in 1930, a house of this size would probably have at least two full-time live-in servants.) Up the stairs there were three rooms, each with its own sink and fireplace.

Mrs. Moore and the family made some immediate changes to the house almost straight away. The upstairs rooms were all in a straight line, one on the right of the landing, and one to the left, through which you had to go to get to the third. The plan was for Maureen to have the upstairs bedroom to the right of the landing, and Mrs. Moore to have the one on the left. This meant that Jack would have the one beyond Mrs. Moore's room, but you could not get to that room without going through Mrs. Moore's room. So to avoid that, a steep wooden and steel pipe staircase was built and a door cut through the outside wall to Jack's bedroom so that he could come and go to his bedroom without having to pass through Mrs. Moore's room. This staircase came down right beside the archway that led into the back porch of the house. The only disadvantage to this arrangement was that whoever used that room, in this case Jack, had to go outside to get to his bedroom or from his bedroom to the rest of the house, but Jack didn't mind. Also, with all the bedrooms needed for family and staff, there was nowhere for Warnie to live, but as he was still in the army, this was not an immediate problem.

They decided to add two rooms, but when looking at the plans, it turned out that three rooms would be more convenient, so three rooms were put on to the back of the house. Now, as you came into the front door, the corridor led away to the left as well as to the right, and as you went to the left, you immediately turned right again and found a doorway on your left which entered a new bedroom with sink and fireplace, and then farther down the corridor and down two steps was a study with a fireplace and then a small bedroom again with a sink and a fireplace.

When the new rooms were finished, the family had enough space for either two live-in servants; or, if the servants did not live in, two guestrooms and a music room for Maureen who was beginning to show considerable talent as a musician. In the end it was a funny house, all passages and rooms in strange places, typical of the houses Jack and Warnie had always lived in, but it was comfortable. The house was heated and supplied with hot water by a big old-fashioned boiler in the kitchen that burned coal or wood, as did all the fireplaces, and the kitchen was equipped with a big Aga cooking stove. Agas were designed in Sweden by a blind man who was a genius at design; they are world famous and still produced to this day. In fact, if you visit The Kilns today, you will find that it is still equipped with an Aga cooker, one that the Aga company kindly provided to the restorers, The C. S. Lewis Foundation of Redlands,

California, who have brought the house back into the style that it was when Jack lived there.

∞

The next major job after buying the house was moving into it. By this time the family had bought a car, a Jowett. They were all learning to drive it, and as Warnie sardonically remarked, "It must be a pretty sturdy car." Fortunately for the health and welfare of the public at large, it wasn't long before Jack decided that he would never be any good as a driver and gave up any attempt to learn the mechanical art of piloting a motorized wheeled conveyance. Maureen on the other hand was soon quite good at it. Jack was expected to be too busy at college to be involved in the move, so Warnie went along to help. Warnie had his own motorcycle and sidecar, a make known as a Daudel, and much preferred this means of transport to cars. However, when Warnie arrived at Hillsboro, the place where the family was living in Oxford, much to his complete astonishment he found Jack seated in the driver's seat of the car all ready to drive up to The Kilns. Warnie was surprised to find Jack there at all, but he was amazed and perhaps a little alarmed to find him about to drive a car. Jack drove carefully with a kind of desperate concentration but eventually arrived at the new house safely. It was, however, the last time he ever attempted to drive. The Kilns was full of bits and pieces of furniture all over the place, so the family worked hard until it all came into some semblance of order.

Finally, for the first time, the family settled into a home of their own, and what a home it was. In the first year of their living there, Jack and Warnie planted hundreds of trees throughout the gardens and on the land up the hill, trees which were later to make the grounds of The Kilns into the stunningly lovely place that they became. The Kilns suited the family admirably, being private and yet not too isolated, within comfortable walking distance of Jack's rooms at Magdalen. It was quiet and yet filled all summer with the music of the English song-birds, especially in the evenings and in that magical time just before dawn. It was a heaven for both Jack and Warnie and a glorious home for Maureen. Mrs. Moore also loved the place. Now, in a country retreat of their own, the family would begin a new life.

Mrs. Moore at last had a roof over her head that she could call her own and, more important to her, a proper home for her daughter. Mrs. Moore had fled from a broken marriage and had been left totally isolated by the death of her son Paddy. She had moved from place to place living in rented and often crowded accommodations, always poor and always insecure. Now at last she could begin a life of some emotional security with the warmth of her unofficially adopted son and her daughter around her and also, when he was on leave from the army, Warnie. Maureen at last had her own bedroom and a settled family atmosphere in which to grow-up. She had a home to which she could bring her friends and of which she could be proud and where she could feel safe and comfortable. Warnie now had, at last, somewhere to go home when he was on leave, a wondrously beautiful place that he could think and dream about when he was stationed at Bulford or later on at Shanghai, China—his own place where his own bedroom and study were waiting for him.

Here at The Kilns Jack would at long last start his real life, his serious writing career, and his settled domesticity as a bachelor university teacher. And more important than anything else that ever happened to him, it was here that he began his long and eventful walk with Jesus Christ.

Chapter Six

FRIENDS AND FAMILY

We have to look back a bit now to those difficult years before the family moved to The Kilns to really get the hang of how Jack was changing and growing as a personality.

Jack came out of the army in 1919 after his service in the war and started back at Oxford. In 1921 he had already established himself as accepting responsibility for Mrs. Moore and Maureen and by the summer of that year had left his college student lodgings and moved in with them. They had already moved from Bristol to Oxford to be near him.

In this year, too, Albert Lewis finally visited Jack at Oxford. This was a little awkward to say the least because Jack felt that he had to keep it secret that he was living with the Moores because he didn't think his father would approve of him using his allowance to support the family of his friend. Somehow he managed to keep it secret, and it seems Albert didn't find out; or at least, if he had found out, he didn't let Jack know.

Jack found that he was able to settle into the everyday work of a household with an ease that surprised him, despite the fact that he did not enjoy many of the chores that he found became necessary for him. He had to study for exams and at the same time try to help run a household. Jack had never really been in this sort of situation before. At home there had always been servants; at school he had been looked after, more or less. In the army he had been an officer and thus had always had a servant (known in the British Army as a "batman," a word that comes from Mediaeval Latin meaning a man who takes care of the officer's packsaddle and thus his personal gear). Even in college as a student, he had always had a "scout." Suddenly faced with the discovery that vegetables needed to be peeled and dishes washed and that this sort of thing might as well be done by him as by anyone else in the family came as something of a shock to him. Nevertheless, he just set to and did whatever came to his hand.

It was also something of a new and unusual experience for Jack to be sharing his home with women. Mrs. Moore was old enough to be his mother and treated him very much as if she were, and Maureen was a lively fourteen-year-old at the time. Jack himself was a mere twenty-three, but even so, he was the head of the household, and he and Mrs. Moore did most of the work. It was Jack who attended Maureen's school plays and sports days, and it was Jack who provided most of the finances for the family. There is no one thing better designed to grow someone up quickly and thoroughly than to accept and to see through a large burden of responsibility, and that was exactly what Jack had done.

In between his studies and the household chores, Jack was trying his hand at writing more poetry. In fact, on the morning of Sunday, April 2, 1922, a fine, sunny spring day, while Mrs. Moore was in the kitchen of their rented house cutting up oranges for marmalade, Jack was sitting in his bedroom by an open window, writing the beginning of what was to be his second published book.

This was an epic poem in rhyme royal called *Dymer*.

It is hard to understand how Jack managed to take care of the chores, forge ahead with his studies, and write poetry all at the same time; and it is even harder to understand how he managed to read the really extraordinary amount of literature that he did. All day everyday there were endless little jobs that he was called on to do. Washing the dishes, mopping floors, sweeping, painting, laying linoleum, hanging curtains, taking the dog out for a walk, tutoring a succession of young women (to raise extra money), and constantly trying to entertain the paying guests whom Mrs. Moore took in (also to raise money) and the nonpaying ones whom were there as a result of Mrs. Moore's charitable nature.

It seems that his life was spent constantly trying to prevent Mrs. Moore from overworking, something of which I fear there was no real danger. Mrs. Moore seems to have been one of those people who can take a minor household job such as making marmalade and turn it into a major labor. She is recorded as having spent four days making marmalade on one occasion, a job that shouldn't take more than a day. She evidently needed to feel that she was constantly the center of attention of those around her and was always having "accidents" and mishaps that drew everyone in the house to her side to make sure that she was all right. When she had achieved this, she would then assume an air of long-suffering and protest that she was all right and that they shouldn't fuss over her while in fact this was exactly what she wanted them to do.

I suppose, to be fair, we should remember that she had been married to a man whom she referred to as "The Beast" for whatever reasons and then had lost her beloved son in the war. She must have felt desperately alone, and when you feel like that, you need to be reminded that there are people around who care for you. It is an easy trap to fall into, that of making things happen to reassure yourself that people do care and will come rushing to aid you if anything goes wrong. She made sure that things went wrong all the time and ran Jack, and to a lesser degree Maureen, ragged trying to look after her.

Jack would be writing or studying in his room when he would suddenly hear a terrible crash from somewhere downstairs and a plaintive cry from Mrs. Moore. In great anxiety he would run down to find that she had tripped over something and was not in the least hurt but very "shaken." Jack would bustle about setting all to rights again and then return to his work, only to be summoned again ten minutes later to go out and buy something or to perform some other minor and largely unnecessary task. This was the sort of thing that happened whenever they were without visitors in the house, which was seldom enough. When there were visitors, Mrs. Moore was utterly charming to them but all the while would grumble about them to Jack whenever they were not present and make a fuss about the huge amount of work they caused her, much of which Jack himself actually did.

The family was always short of money, and this was a constant source of worry for Jack. Mrs. Moore's husband sent her some (they were legally separated and he was legally bound to do so), and Jack's University allowance from his father also contributed to the family finances. It was never enough. They moved from house to house and from flat to flat. Whenever they were living somewhere with enough room, Mrs. Moore would find some young woman or young man to come and live with them who would pay for board and lodging, and this would help a bit more.

Maureen was attending Headington School and also taking music lessons, and it was always difficult to find enough money to pay for this. She also brought her young friends home, and Mrs. Moore would always find them something to eat and make a fuss over them, but afterward she would complain to Jack about the expense and the work.

To make things worse, Mrs. Moore was always suffering from some kind of illness or other and had to be looked after all the time. If she did not have a toothache, she had a headache; if she did not have a headache, she had rheumatism; if it was not rheumatism, it was sciatica, and so on and so forth. Jack himself was genuinely in delicate health during these years, but I suppose that was to be expected. He had lived in foul, infectious mud infested with rats and disease-carrying lice for half a year and then been blown up and spent months in the hospital. It takes years to recover fully from something like that.

He also was plagued with nightmares, many about the war but many others of all kinds too, and rarely enjoyed a good night's sleep. I have a theory about Jack's nightmares, which I thought out when I lived with him. Jack lived almost all his life in houses that were very cold, particularly at night. Now I don't know if you have ever tried to sleep in a very cold place; but without any heating at all, it is quite natural that you try to burrow under the covers of your bed in an effort to keep warm. Jack developed the habit of sleeping covered right up with even his head under the covers. In this position it is hard to get fresh air to breathe, and soon you are breathing air that you have already breathed before and from which you have already taken most of the oxygen. When this happens, nightmares almost always start. Jack was frequently up late at night finishing off his chores and studying and would often be wakened during the night with his own nightmares or Mrs. Moore's illnesses, which demanded that he get up from his own bed to prepare her a hot water bottle or some hot milk or something. Then he would be up early in the morning to get the house ready for the day, lighting the fires and boiling the kettle or whatever was required.

Years later I became aware that Warnie liked and admired Mrs. Moore at first; but after he joined the household of The Kilns, when he retired from the army, he slowly began to detest her. She treated Jack as though he was her personal slave, and this Warnie found insufferable. After some years Warnie asked Jack why he put up with it all the time, but Jack simply told him politely to mind his own business.

It is often said that you never really know someone until you actually live with them, and I think it is true. Mrs. Moore was charming and pleasant to all Jack's friends who visited them, and they all liked her immensely. In her own home and to her family, she was a gentle but manipulative tyrant, always making sure that she got whatever she wanted and yet always pretending to be everybody's servant and always letting them know it.

Many strange people came through their homes during those years, most of them young women who came as guests (paying or otherwise), as pupils for Jack to teach, or as friends of Maureen or Mrs. Moore; but the strangest of all was Mrs. Moore's brother. He was a doctor and was always referred to as simply "The Doc." He was a welcome guest for some years as also was his American wife; but slowly, as time passed, he began to get peculiar. He was interested in spiritualism and the occult and was experimenting with those dangerous and foolish things and was gradually going stark raving mad. It was (it seems almost inevitably) while he was staying with Jack and Mrs. Moore that he finally flipped out completely and went utterly bonkers. Jack was the one who held him down when he began to scream and talked him back to sense again and again. Jack spent night after night with him, sharing the watches with Mrs. Moore and always being called if The Doc began to have "the horrors" during Mrs. Moore's shift. Jack worried not only about The Doc but also about Mrs. Moore. They sensibly sent Maureen away to stay with friends while this was all going on. Finally The Doc was committed to a psychiatric hospital, and he died there a while later. This whole episode sapped Jack's strength and frightened him badly. He had nightmares about it for years afterward.

As I have said, Jack was often ill during these years, and yet he still worked on tirelessly at all the tasks he regarded as his duty. To understand this we have to look at what sort of man Jack was becoming. He had read and had been greatly impressed by all the books about knights in armor, all the myths about heroes and men who put their duty before their personal safety, comfort, or convenience, and he had begun to believe, and quite rightly, that this was indeed the right way for a man to think and to behave. It was largely for this reason that he fought in the war when he could have avoided it. He simply felt that it was his duty. He had developed a high regard for the concept of honor, and this is something that seems inherent in all men in one way or another. It is often twisted and mis-placed but still seems to emerge in the oddest of people and the oddest of places. Having found this idea of honor, Jack pursued it in his reading in order to find out what it

really meant and what it should be. As a result he had
worked out exactly where duty and honor fit into the
making of a man; and having done so, he then set out to
live by the code of chivalry he had worked out for himself.
He never expected others to live by his own personal code,
but he was often disappointed that people seemed to care
nothing for the ideas themselves. Jack had made a promise to Paddy, and he intended to see it thorough till the
very end, and he did.

Often enough Jack was sick and depressed, but he
didn't allow that to slow him down or to affect his
relationships with other people. He frequently had bad
headaches but told no one and simply worked on regard-
less. His digestion was poor, probably damaged by the disease and poor food that he suffered in the war and then by
the poverty diet that he had to live on during this trying
and worry-filled ten years. The worry itself would not have
helped either; he was always worried about not having
enough money to look after his "family" properly. He was
living in a household, or rather a succession of house-
holds that were full of tension and difficulty, never knowing how long they were going to be able to stay in any one
home. Often there were strangers living with them, and
this is always difficult for people who are by nature shy
and private as indeed Jack was. It was made especially difficult for him because it often fell to him to entertain and
look after these young women. He tried to keep the peace
between Mrs. Moore and Maureen, who in typical teenage
fashion was beginning to think she knew everything and
was rude and rebellious toward her mother. Jack worried
too about the fact that despite his excellent scholastic
record he simply could not find a job. He applied again
and again for fellowships to various colleges but again and
again saw men less well qualified than himself appointed

in his place. He had to wait until 1925 to finally get a real job at Magdalen College.

It added to Jack's discomfiture that several of the young women who came to live with them during this time, or whom he had to teach, fell in love with him. Most were soon discouraged when they were made aware that he did not return their affections and behaved very well, but one in particular simply wouldn't give up and made Jack's life difficult by pretending to faint every now and then and being generally lovesick for a long time.

One most important source of trouble for Jack was the fact that he felt he had to keep his adoption of the Moore family a secret from his father. Albert was generous in keeping Jack's allowance going all this time, but he could not have done so if he had openly known that Jack was using it to support an unofficial family. I am almost sure that Albert knew well how Jack was spending his allowance and how he was living but turned a blind eye to it all. If some interfering busybody of a relative or family friend had officially told him, he would have been forced by convention to do something about it such as cutting off Jack's allowance. This would have been a catastrophe for Jack and for Mrs. Moore and Maureen, and it was made all the more nerve-racking for Jack by the fact that his Aunt Lily lived close to them most of the time.

Aunt Lily herself was a peculiar woman, and Jack visited her often, as it was his duty to do so. He did not enjoy the visits, and they always left him exhausted and depressed. The smell of cats always reminded him of his Aunt Lily, as she lived with every stray cat she could get her hands on and frequently adopted more. She was known by the local people as "that lady with all them cats."

As time went by, life became steadily more difficult to bear. He was passed over for job after job. Mrs. Moore steadily became more and more demanding and hired

maid after maid, in whom she soon found fault and none
of whom stayed long. When they left in what is called
"high dudgeon" or in a flood of tears, Jack had to take
over the work. Maureen, as she grew older, found it more
and more difficult to accept her mother's domination and
became more argumentative; and this led to domestic
rows that upset Mrs. Moore so much that she would
instantly become ill, and once again the burden of work
would fall to Jack. The visitors who came to stay seem to
have gone from a bit odd to decidedly peculiar and in
some cases absolutely horrible, and Jack always seemed to
get the task of attending to their needs or indeed of telling
them that they simply must learn how to behave themselves. How Jack stood it all is a mystery, but he did have
a couple of valuable safeguards.

The first was the company and society of some of the
men he met and began to know at Oxford University—
men whose minds were clear and enquiring, whose conversation was stimulating and whose company he began
to enjoy. There were also many who were boring of course,
but Jack slowly built up around him a group of valuable
acquaintances, some of whom began to become friends.
Now friendship in those days was a bit different from
what it is today; friends did not have to agree on everything and often agreed on practically nothing. They were
people with whom you could argue all day and yet never
get irritated or angry at all. In today's world we seem to
have lost the real meaning of friendship. If someone dis-
agrees with us, it is fashionable today to dislike them for
it. This is silly and robs us of the best kind of friends we
could find, for if we are always agreed with, we can never
really have a serious conversation; we cannot learn from
someone who agrees with what we say. The men who
began to be Jack's friends would be his friends for the rest
of his life, men like J. R. R. Tolkien, Owen Barfield, Leo

Baker, and Alfred Harwood. These men and their conversation were a kind of safety net for Jack throughout these long troubling years.

Another life raft for Jack was the fact that he could get away for long walks, which came under the heading of "exercise." He was a fast and determined walker, and he strode through the countryside for miles every day. He learned the difference between daydreams and thought while on his walks and then talked about it with his friends. They called the idle daydreams "Christina Dreams" after a character in a book. He thought and walked and read and walked and sometimes even wrote and walked, making up lines in his head and then stopping for a while to write them down in a notebook. Jack walked for exercise of both mind and body, and he learned again to love the sights, sounds, and smells of the countryside in which he was walking. He walked in all kinds of weathers and conditions, reveling as much in rain as he did in sunshine, in mud as much as in good, hard, solid going. He spared himself only an hour or so for walking in the hard times, but later and on his rare holidays, he would spend all day out among the woods and fields, covering mile after mile of country. To his great joy he found that some of his friends were enthusiastic walkers as well, and some of their best conversations were held while resting during their marches across hills and valleys. It was a pleasure that he continued almost all his life.

So here we have a young man who after going through hell and being very ill for a long time, accepted a huge task, that of taking care of a family (which was not even his own) with never enough money, never knowing for sure that they would have a roof over their heads or enough food to eat. To get a good idea of how much this

terms. For them there was no Little Lea any more, no Albert, and in a sense even Ireland itself would never be the same for them. They would never go home to it again. It was all over, finished, ended. Whatever happened now would be theirs and theirs alone for better or worse.

And so to The Kilns, and at once Jack and Warnie set about making the gardens and the woods as beautiful as they could become. Jack was thirty-two years old and Warnie thirty-five, and thus they were at the prime of their lives both physically and mentally, and they started to work on the gardens and the grounds as soon as they could.

At this stage Warnie was still a regular army officer and was only able to be at The Kilns on weekends, but when he was there, he joined in with Jack on all sorts of projects aimed at making the place as wonderful as they knew it could be. The lake had developed a heavy growth of various waterweeds which all but completely choked the water, so Jack and Warnie took the punt, which had come with the place, and started to pull out the weeds and ferry them to shore. A punt is a flat-bottomed boat about twelve or fourteen feet long and maybe as much as four feet wide and is propelled by pushing it along with a pole that you push against the bottom. There is a lot of skill involved in this, and beginners sometimes find themselves getting the pole stuck in the bottom. This can be funny, especially if the beginner doesn't let go of the pole because all of a sudden the punt moves off and then you are left clinging to a pole stuck in the bottom of the lake or river. It slowly falls over, and splash, down you go. Warnie became good at punting, but Jack was always more inclined just to use a paddle to move the boat.

They would set out from shore and heave great masses of weed into the punt with rakes and forks, then pole over to the bank and pitchfork the evil-smelling muddy mass ashore. The punt soon became covered in the black ooze from the lake bottom, and the two of them got wet, smelly, and muddy during the day. It was warm work too, and although they didn't really enjoy it very much, they were glad to see the clear water slowly taking over from the weeds. Being at the bottom of a hillside, mud and rotting vegetation from the woods flowed down into the lake whenever it rained and slowly silted it up. The weeds then grew in the rich mud on the bottom, and lots of it came up into the punt as they hauled in their cargo of wild water lilies and the other slimy green stuff that was taking over the lake.

One day a neighbor and friend of Mrs. Moore's came to visit and insisted that Jack take her out in the punt. Luckily this lady, a certain Mrs. Armitage, had a good sense of humor because Jack got them out into the middle of the lake and then found that he couldn't get the punt to go in the right direction. As I said, Jack was never good with the pole. Soon the two of them with The Kilns dog, Mr. Papworth, were out in the middle, and the punt was slowly spinning around and around going nowhere. Mr. Papworth was barking, and in the general confusion Mrs. Armitage slipped and fell down into the punt and into the inches-thick layer of slimy black mud in the bottom of it, displaying to the world her bright red knickers. Warnie stood on the bank in helpless laughter, and Mrs. Armitage was also in stitches. Poor Jack was terribly embarrassed, but he too saw the funny side of it afterward. When they finally got close to shore, Mr. Papworth showed his disregard of Jack's skills by leaping ashore as soon as he thought he could make it and, with a disapproving glare in Jack's direction, took off for home.

On another occasion Jack got his revenge. One day when he and Warnie were hard at work forking weeds from the punt to the bank, Warnie miscalculated his swing withthe fork, and his pitchfork load of weeds, instead of flying gracefully to the bank, went straight up in the air and came down on top of his head, crowning him with a smelly garland of slimy weeds oozing black mud. Jack laughed till he cried, and Warnie had to retire to the house to wash.

Over the summer that first year, they managed to clear all the weeds out of the lake and were able to go swimming. Swimming in the lake was interesting because there were two springs at the bottom of it, one at the western end and one in the middle, and you always knew when you were over the springs because the water suddenly got cold. The lake was deep enough to swim from one side to the other and from end to end. Now, after seventy years, the steady silting up of the lake has resulted in most of it being far too shallow to swim in; and even though it was dredged out a bit a few years ago, it is still nothing like it was in Jack and Warnie's early days there, or even in the late 1950s and early '60s when I used to swim in it.

Jack and Warnie were at last able to spend more time together than they had for many years, not since they were at school in fact, and they were thus able to renew the closeness of their boyhood relationship. They worked together, Warnie sharing Jack's rooms at Magdalen, while he was working at editing the family papers, and Jack working at his studies for future writings and his duties as a fellow of the college. They worked together on the gardens and grounds of The Kilns, weeded the lake together, sawed up firewood together, planted trees together, and generally worked at getting to know each other properly again. Warnie still had to be on duty for most of each week, but his weekends were mostly his own, and he joined in the family life enthusiastically. He already found Mrs. Moore's habit of using Jack's time as if he were a domestic servant a little irritating. He thought it an awful waste for someone as brilliant as his younger brother to be washing dishes and peeling vegetables, but he just put up with it and spent as much time with Jack as he could. Jack even managed to persuade Warnie (who was neither athletic nor energetic) to join him on a walking tour, something Warnie had never done before. In 1931 they took the train to Chepstow and then walked back, covering fifty-four miles in four days. Warnie said later that it was the best holiday he had ever had in his life.

Warnie also joined in doing some of the household chores. Someone had given them a pair of swans for the lake; Warnie sometimes fed these as well as the household chickens, and he often took Mr. Papworth for walks. All this time both Jack and Warnie were coming more and more under the spell which the beauty of The Kilns used to be able to cast over all who went there. During 1931 the two brothers planted forty-three trees, and some of them are still there to this day. All this time of course, they both knew that Warnie would have to do one more overseas stint in the army before he retired, but by now Warnie knew too that the home that had faded and gone with the death of their father had well and truly been replaced with a new and better one. The Kilns was now home, their home, and so a certain security entered both of their lives.

∞

By this time Warnie too had made his own journey of discovery from not caring, to not believing in anything very much, to definitely not believing in God, and then finally, as he learned more from both his own life and his studies of the lives of others, to truth and Christianity. Thus finally, the two brothers were once more close friends and sharing the same convictions that Jesus is God and deserving of our worship.

In the summer of 1931, Warnie described The Kilns as "a veritable garden of Eden, a lotus island, a faerie land, or any other term which will express sheer loveliness." And so it was, and the memory of it is burned in beauty deep in my mind.

∞

For Jack also this first year at The Kilns was one of delight and finally a feeling of safety. He had secured a good job with long-term prospects, was coming into the full flower of his writing talent, and had the education and experience to make it work. He had lost one family but had been adopted into another; he had lost one home but had at last found another. And his brother, the companion of his life, was returning to him after years of trouble and separation for them both.

Jack didn't mind all the chores and difficulties that surrounded him. He could escape to college when he needed to, and after years of poverty he was grateful that he was now able to earn enough money to provide for his family. He was not rich by any means, but at least he did not have to scrimp and save for everything he needed. He could buy the necessities and an occasional luxury. He still worried about money though because the habit was so ingrained into him that although he had no need to fear he was unable to stop doing so. This unreasoning fear of poverty lasted all his life and prevented him from ever really enjoying his position in life. As they all sorted themselves out and really began to settle into The Kilns, it soon became apparent to Jack that he had found a home he could (and would) grow to love. In summer the place was almost indescribably beautiful, and in winter a good fall of snow turned it into a faerie land of glowing white and sparkling frost.

There was work to be done for sure, but it was work that was such a change from his everyday activities that Jack loved it. Slipping and sliding around in the weeds and mud from the lake, planting trees, sawing up fallen ones for firewood, and all the outdoor jobs that he found waiting for him, he discovered to be a wonderful change from the daily grind of indoor chores and the study, teaching, and writing that were his usual work. No matter how good we are at our special work, we need to take breaks from it and do something completely different every now and then. It is vital to our health—mental, physical, and emotional. This and more Jack was now discovering for himself.

It made a huge difference in his life to have his own home and one where the family for which he had assumed full responsibility could feel free of the worry of having to move on. It also made a big difference to him to be able to invite his friends out to his home and to see them filled with admiration for the place and its potential. Jack was becoming a man of substance.

Soon the family found a man who was to become a member of the household for more than thirty years and was to be a strong influence on all of them. The man they had hired to help in the gardens and to drive their car—his name was Lyddiatt—had left, and a replacement had to be found. The man they hired was to be the basis of several characters in Jack's later books. His name was Frederick Paxford. Paxford (as he was almost always called), a bachelor, was a wonderful and extraordinary man. He came from Oxfordshire country stock and was as honest as the day is long in summertime. He spoke with a slow, burring Cotswold drawl; and if he could find nothing good to say about someone, he said nothing about them at all. Paxford had been a soldier in the war, had been poisoned by poison gas, and had spent months recovering his strength. He was a genius at mechanical things; he could see with a sort of uncanny sixth sense how a machine worked and what was wrong with it. In those days The Kilns had its own electricity generator powered by a petrol engine down in the garage, and it was a cranky piece of equipment. A small motor drove a generator that charged a series of large batteries. These were lead-acid batteries in big glass jars, and when they were charging, they fizzed and bubbled and shot out tiny drops of acid, which ate holes in your shirt. Warnie told me years later that Paxford was the only man who could make it work reliably, and he still wore shirts with tiny holes in them from his days of tending this acid-spitting creature.

He drove cars steadily and well and could be trusted with any task to which you put him. He was also a man who had been brought up with strong principles, and honesty and loyalty were two things that he loved and admired and stuck to all his life. He had a sense of economy that was both valuable and at times infuriating, as he always did the household shopping and always made sure that there was never more than precisely enough of anything in the house. Like most country folk he loved the soil and growing things and had a deep understanding of gardening and everything to do with plants and gardens. Quiet and unassuming, he seemed to have friends everywhere he went. A shopping trip on his bike took Paxford half the day, even if he only had to go to Headington, because he had to stop and chat with people who knew and liked him every few minutes. Paxford was the same age as Jack, and joining The Kilns household in the multiple roles of gardener, handyman, and chauffeur was the start of a new life for him also.

Years later he became my best friend and support, after Jack himself, and I was honored to be asked by him to use his Christian name and call him Fred.

There was an enormous amount of work to be done at The Kilns, particularly in those early years, and Paxford joined in with a hearty will. He helped to clear and then develop the gardens and planted trees in the woods. He grew a wide variety of "vegebles," as he called them in the garden and took over the old greenhouse for tomatoes and other vegetables. Mrs. Moore was keen on home-grown vegetables and also kept chickens to supply the house with eggs, and they soon became part of Paxford's responsibilities.

One of the things that made Paxford extraordinary was that once he had learned something he always thought it was right, no matter where he had learned it, and it was difficult to change his mind about anything. He had ideas about everything, and Mrs. Moore soon began to place more trust in his ideas than was reasonable. "Paxford says" became her catch-cry for information about almost anything. Much of it was wrong, but she believed everything he told her. A less honest man and one with less integrity could have taken advantage of this, but Paxford never did. It began to annoy Warnie to be told that he was wrong about something that he really did know about simply because "Paxford said," and because of this he had to fight against the temptation to begin unfairly to dislike Paxford.

Fred Paxford had an amazing language skill, which seems to have been peculiar to him alone. He used the word *ah* in almost every sentence, and with minor changes in tone or inflection managed to make it mean "yes," "no," "maybe," "hello," "goodbye," and various other things. It took me a long while to fathom them all and to be able to know that I really understood him. Jack was able to do this too, but Warnie never got the hang of it.

Another fact of his personality was that he was always ready to say the most depressing things and apparently to take the gloomiest attitude to everything while at the same time to expect everything to turn out well. I have a sneaking suspicion that he voiced the worst possible thoughts about things to protect himself and others from their actually happening. About the punt he would say, "Ah, y' wants ter be careful, them sinks yer know," as if by saying it and calling everyone's attention to the possibility, he was somehow ensuring that it wouldn't happen. Jack and Warnie told me of one occasion in spring when the time came to bring the punt out of its winter storage in the barn, paint it, and put it back in the lake. Fred painted the punt, and then they waited for the paint to dry so that they could use the punt. Every time they asked Paxford if the punt was dry, he simply replied, "Nah, 'er b'aint droi yet." Finally, in exasperation Warnie said, "Well, when will it be dry?" To which Paxford replied, "Well sir, there be a lot o' oil in that paint; 'er moight never be droi." It was not that Paxford was in the least bit lazy, but he never believed in doing anything until it had to be done. He knew that when the paint was dry, he would have to help take the punt up to the lake and launch it, so he was putting the job off until it could no longer be avoided. But he was right, the paint was still sticky, and they all got it on their hands and clothes when they launched the punt.

Paxford soon had rows and rows of "vegebles" in the garden, an orchard planted, and flower beds all arranged and growing well. The Kilns became more and more the beautiful place that Jack and Warnie had imagined, and a lot of the credit must go to Fred Paxford. This big strong countryman had other talents too. He was fond of singing and, as he went about his garden duties, would sing loudly and (until he got rather deaf later in life from after-effects of the gas poisoning) quite tunefully, songs that he had known and loved in his youth. This gave rise to one of the most amusing (or, to Warnie, most annoying) things about him many years later, but we'll come to that much later in the story. He was also a good cook and would take over the kitchen when the maid or Mrs. Moore wanted to take a day off. His duties also included looking after the Aga cooking stove and the old boiler that heated the hot water and the central heating for the house. Fred didn't actually sleep in the house, though he ate all his meals there. He had his own little private bungalow in the garden, which was his personal place, and he was to live there for the next thirty-three years.

The household at The Kilns was now almost complete. Warnie didn't live there yet because he was still in the army and had to live wherever he was posted, only coming home at the weekends, but the rest of the family was now comfortably installed in their new home.

The household now consisted of Mrs. Moore, Jack (who slept in college during term time and was home at night only on weekends), Maureen, a maid (though maids came and went quite often), Fred Paxford, and later a housekeeper called Vera Henry. This soon sorted itself out into a balanced and well-run home, in which all the grown-ups had their regular duties and in which Jack did any extra work that needed to be done. Paxford's joining them was a great gift for Jack, as it meant there was someone to take a lot of chores off his shoulders and to do as a matter of daily duty a lot of jobs that Jack had had to do whenever he got the chance.

∞

Soon a kind of routine was worked out and life almost settled into a pattern, though it was never very sure and things changed from day to day. In the vacations Mrs. Moore or Jack would get up early and make a pot of tea to start the day, and then Mrs. Moore would prepare breakfast for the household. At around eight o'clock, breakfast was usually ready unless something had gone wrong, as it often did. The family would eat in the dining room; and the staff, the housekeeper (when there was one), maid, and Paxford would eat in the kitchen. After breakfast and washing up, which was done either by the maid (if they had one at the time) or Jack, Maureen would go off to school or during holidays would pursue her own interests, and Jack would retire to his study to work and/or read and study. Mrs. Moore and the maid would then clean the house and prepare the lunch. At around eleven o'clock either Mrs. Moore or the maid would bring Jack a cup of tea and a few biscuits. Mrs. Moore would sit with him and have a cup of tea as well. And then he would return to his work and she to hers. At about twelve or one o'clock—or later or earlier, you never could tell—lunch would be served in the dining room for the family; the staff would have theirs in the kitchen. After washing up was done, Jack would set out for a walk and return to tea at about four. Tea would be a pot of tea and a few biscuits or a piece of cake, and then he would go back to his work, and Mrs. Moore would continue with her work of running the household and preparing dinner. Dinner was supposed to be served at around eight o'clock and sometimes was, though it was often later; and then they would sit and talk or entertain whatever guests were there until bedtime.

Throughout the day, every day, Mrs. Moore would frequently and repeatedly call Jack to help with hundreds of little jobs around the house, many of them unnecessary and some of them just made-up work, and he would patiently put down his pen or book and go to peel vegetables or sweep up something spilled in the kitchen or clean something or whatever and then return to take up where he had left off. This routine, changing a little as circumstances changed, but not very much, went on for almost twenty years. Maureen grew up and eventually got married and left, and Mrs. Moore grew old and ever more crotchety. Warnie joined the household as soon as he retired and became a full-time resident at The Kilns, but Jack simply settled down and became a writer and teacher.

The world went to war again much later, and we will come to that in a bit. Warnie went from loving the house and the household to becoming slowly irritated by it and eventually to loathing every nook and cranny of the place, poisoned for him by Mrs. Moore and her proprietary attitude toward Jack. He did not begin to love The Kilns again until Mrs. Moore had gone into a nursing home many years later. The ones who never really changed at all, except to get older and wiser, were Jack and Paxford.

The Lewis family.

Lewis as a young boy, photographed with a favorite toy.

C. S. Lewis and Warren Lewis as children.

The Lewis family and staff on Little Lea steps. Little Lea was the name given to the Lewis's house in Hillsborough.

C. S. Lewis in 1919 at the age of twenty-one.

C. S. Lewis and good friend, Paddy Moore.

Lewis with the O.T.C. cadet group during his service in World War I.

C. S. Lewis with his father, Albert.

Lewis as student at Oxford in 1919.

Lewis in the Little End Room.

Lewis with Magdalen College faculty. Lewis is in the top row, third from the left.

Lewis, Maureen, and Mrs. Janie Moore.

C. S. Lewis, Mrs. Moore, and Warren at The Kilns.

Distant shot of The Kilns.

C. S. Lewis and his brother Warren.

Lewis in his middle years.

C. S. Lewis at Stonehenge.

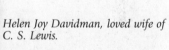

C. S. Lewis, and David and Douglas Gresham.

Helen Joy Davidman, loved wife of C. S. Lewis.

Members of the Inklings (l to r): Commander Jim Dundas-Grant, Colin Hardie, Dr. H. E. "Humphrey" Harvard, and Lewis.

Most famous image of C. S. Lewis.

Chapter Eight

FRIENDS AND GOOD

FELLOWSHIP

In 1931, John Ronald Reuel Tolkien, professor of Anglo-Saxon at Oxford, began to make a habit of calling in to Jack's rooms at Magdalen every Monday morning to spend an hour or two with Jack. The two would read their poems or stories to each other, criticize each other's work, share a pint or two of beer or a pot of tea, and generally simply converse. They talked of many things—of books, of ancient lore, and of myths and kings. Eventually Tolkien invited a friend to come along with him to Jack's rooms, and then Jack invited another to join them. Soon enough a sort of loose gathering of men was making a regular thing of grouping together on Monday mornings: Arthur Owen Barfield, Henry Victor Dyson, Robert Emlyn Havard, Charles Williams, Neville Coghill, Lord David Cecil—all men Jack met in these early years and who became his friends. There were many others too. Some of them went on to become famous writers themselves, like J. R. R. Tolkien and Neville Coghill. Others never became famous, but when Jack made a friend, the friendship was a valued and lasting thing, and many of these men were Jack's friends for the rest of his life.

For Jack, friendship was something of great importance. It usually (but not always) started with the simple recognition of the fact that there was something in which both people were deeply interested, like with his friend from childhood, Arthur Greeves. That friendship began when Jack and Arthur suddenly realized that they were both fascinated by the Norse myths and other books of the same kind. There was always something that they shared, whether an interest in books, ideas, or simply the pleasures of walking, talking, and sharing good fellowship at pubs and inns around the country.

Jack was not really a "club" minded person, but he joined a selection of clubs and societies at the university in order to spend time with people who were interested in, and could talk about, the same things that he himself enjoyed. Jack was wary of membership for its own sake. It was only natural to meet others of the same interests at these special societies, and that indeed was his only motive for joining them. After all, if you were interested in collecting stamps, you would expect to find other people who were also interested in collecting stamps at a stamp collector's club. Jack soon built up a circle of friends around him who all liked to talk of the same sorts of things that he did, and so a sort of loose literary society was formed. It had no written rules or constitution, but for all that it was a close-knit group. It was called "The Inklings," but even that was not in any way a formal name for it. The word *inkling* means a sort of vague idea. If someone asks you a question and you don't have any idea of the answer, you might say, "I don't have the faintest inkling." It also could mean someone who plays with ink, and back in those days writing was done with a pen made of a wooden handle with a steel nib attached to it. You dipped your nib into a bottle of ink or an inkwell and then wrote until the ink on the nib ran out, usually about six or seven words. Then you dipped again.

This is how I learned to write at school, and as crude as it sounds, there were distinct advantages to this system. You had to pause every few seconds to dip your pen in the bottle of ink, and this gave you time to reflect and think about what you were writing. Nowadays with ballpoint pens that last for ages and even more with typewriters and computer keyboards, people often write away without thinking enough about what they are saying. Anyway, Jack and his friends called themselves the Inklings and began to get in the habit of meeting twice a week in order to talk and just generally enjoy the society of men of like minds; and quite early on they moved their morning meetings from Mondays to Tuesdays.

Inklings meetings were soon held on Thursday evenings in Jack's rooms at Magdalen College and on Tuesday afternoons at one or another of the pubs that abound in Oxford and Headington. One pub which has become famous for their meetings was The Eagle and Child, more often known as The Bird and Baby or to Jack and his friends, simply The Bird. It was one that they used often, but they met at others as well. They would decide on Thursday evenings at which pub they would meet the following Tuesday. The Bird and Baby had one distinct advantage for some years though: it had a private back room which the landlord let the group take over as their own for their meetings. Later a new landlord took over, and he changed his pub and did away with the little back room, so they changed their pub and went elsewhere. It would be possible to write a book about the Inklings (and indeed a chap called Humphrey Carpenter has done just that) and yet not go into detail about more than a small number of the members, for the names and faces changed throughout the thirty or so years of this informal club's existence. However, some of the most important members are those who are remembered least often.

For example, Robert Emlyn Havard, who was a medical doctor and who took care of both Jack's and Tolkien's families, did not leave behind him any great books or literary works and yet was a firm and regular attendee of Inklings meetings.

One facet of these men's personalities was that they often bestowed nicknames on their friends. Havard soon became "Humphrey" or "The U.Q." Humphrey was the most used one, and in fact when he became my doctor years later, it was a long time before I found out that it wasn't his real name. U.Q. started on an occasion when Warnie, who was another regular Inkling, was kept waiting by Humphrey, who was often late, and became irritated. He finally exploded with exasperation and said, "What is the matter with that useless quack?"—a quack being a slang term for a bad doctor or one who pretends to be a doctor but isn't. Jack seized on the nickname "Useless Quack" for Humphrey, and he was often referred to as the U.Q. ever after.

In those days it was customary for friends and colleagues to refer to and call one another by their surnames. Jack might have been called "Lewis" (and sometimes was) if it had not been that Warnie was also a member, so Jack was just Jack and Warnie was either Warnie or Major Lewis or Lewis Major (this last one was a word play on his rank and on the fact that he was older than Jack, and so at school he had been Lewis Major whereas Jack was Lewis Minor). Younger members were usually called by their first names; thus Christopher Tolkien was "Christopher," but to make it plain that they were talking about J. R. R.

rather than Christopher, Inklings would often refer to
J. R. R. as "Tollers."

If you were able to climb into a time machine and
zoom back in time so that you could sit and listen to one
of these meetings, the thing you would first become aware
of would be how much fun these men were having. They
roared with laughter, often at each other's expense, and
they mocked and argued good-naturedly among themselves all the time. Their conversations covered everything
under the sun, and they really enjoyed playing with ideas.
One of the most valuable things of that time (and one
which we have almost entirely lost) was that in those days
nobody felt the least bit of need to dislike or grow angry
with someone simply because they disagreed with them.
These men disagreed with one another about almost
everything but never grew annoyed or felt slighted by one
another. Owen Barfield, for example, became fascinated
with a thing called anthroposophy; and Jack found its
teaching both silly and dangerous. The two men spent
many years arguing back and forth over the subject. They
called this their "Great War," and yet they remained the
closest of friends all of Jack's life.

There was also a serious side to Inklings meetings, and
this was that here, at these completely casual meetings full
of fun and laughter, some of the greatest of modern literature found its first, and very critical, audience. It was here
that Tolkien first read aloud the beginnings of a book that
was to become the renowned *The Lord of the Rings,* and earlier he had read *The Hobbit.* It was here that Neville Coghill
first read some of his famous translations of Chaucer's
Canterbury Tales. Here too Warnie read extracts of his books
on French history, which he began to write when he left the
army, and it was here that C. S. Lewis first revealed something new that he was working on called *The Lion, the Witch
and the Wardrobe.*

The Inklings was a sort of refining furnace for great writings. Chapters would be read aloud and then discussed by all who were present. Well-written, worthwhile material would be joyfully received and praised as it deserved, but bad material would be mercilessly cut to pieces under the withering scorn of some of the greatest literary minds of the twentieth century. It was a brave man who would read his work to the Inklings. It would be safe to say that Jack's writings, those of Tolkien, Warnie, John Wain, and others were hugely improved by being subjected to the discussions of the Inklings, and it was because these were men who could see at once where something was wrong or did not quite fit. They would pick up immediately where a meaning was not quite clear or where the author had made a mistake in grammar, and they would say so, often with delight at being able to catch each other out. Works, which were read in this forum and met with the flame of their refining fire, were left polished and bright, glowing with perfection.

There was no formal membership of this group of friends. If someone had a friend they wanted to bring along to the next meeting, he would suggest his name and see how the others reacted. If the man wasn't regarded as being suitable, that was the end of it; but if he was, the member brought him along to the next meeting, and everyone watched gently to see how he fit in. If he fit well, he would be invited back; if he did not, he wouldn't. It wasn't a men-only society or group, but in those days women with both intellect and learning were not as common as they are today, and it was rare to find one with not only the right interests but also the ability to discuss them. Also, many women were not able to join in the cut and thrust of such conversation with sufficient confidence to allow the menfolk to unbridle their tongues. Most women would have had the men wary of embarrassing them or hurting their feelings, and thus when a woman was present, they would not feel able to launch into the sort of hard and tough talk they so enjoyed. There were some exceptions to this though they were few and far between. Also the men of those times were brought up to believe that women were people whom it was their duty to protect, even or perhaps especially, from themselves (and it isn't at all a bad way to think). They would never have been able to indulge in the verbal fencing that they were so good at if each of them was always trying to protect a member of the group from all the other members of the group.

The Inklings began in a small way, as such groups do, but it grew not so much in numbers as in intensity and importance. Slowly, as the years passed, more and more members came and went. Some were keen students whose minds and interests were such that they were welcomed along to Tuesday meetings, which were more lighthearted than the Thursday night gatherings, and then when they had completed their Oxford studies, they would pass on out into the world. (The Thursday night meetings that took place in Jack's rooms at Magdalen College were often serious explorations of work in progress.) Some were visitors to the university who also came for a time and then went their way. But others there were staunch and true men who came week by week and year by year, and these became a group of friends who would rather spend time together than they would spend time apart. They talked together; some would take holidays together; they would learn and study together; and they would suffer together as the world moved through its inevitable changes. The Inklings became a sort of literary round table.

While all this was happening in Jack's professional life, his family life was slowly changing too. First was the huge change of finding and settling into a real home, The Kilns. But as time passed other more subtle changes happened too. For example, Maureen was steadily growing up. She had been a rebellious thirteen year old when Jack had accepted the responsibility of looking after her and her mother, and she grew more and more into the fairly typical behavior that we have now come to expect from young people as they begin to find their own way in life. It is a difficult time for both the young person and the people trying to teach and guide them. The adults looking back at their own lives see the young person plunging headlong into ideas and actions that they know will be hurtful or even disastrous for the young one and try to forbid these things, or at least advise against them. Youngsters often react against this, as they don't have the experience to see why something they are doing or want to do will be bad for them, and so an argument starts.

Maureen was talented in music and was learning to be a pianist. This was often a source of worry for Mrs. Moore and Jack because they knew that she had the talent, but they never had enough money to pay for really first-class training for her and always felt that they were letting her down. They spent more money than they could really afford to send her to a good school where they thought she would get a good education in all subjects, including music. This turned out not to be quite true, as her piano teaching was not as good as it might have been, and Maureen did not develop as well as she might have with a better teacher.

Mrs. Moore was by nature an outwardly charitable soul, and she often had young friends in some kind of difficulty coming to stay at The Kilns. They would move in full of woes and problems, stabilize themselves a little, and then move on with their lives. Jack built up a circle of friends through this, very different from those friends at the university; but some of these friends, most of them women, also became friends for life. Jack played croquet with them on the lawn at The Kilns and became quite good at it. He also played tennis on the tennis court but was not as good at that game. He took them out on the lake in the punt and for walks around the grounds and up onto Shotover Hill, but he never found himself romantically attracted to any of them, and there were several who regretted that. One or two embarrassed Jack by falling in love with him and making it very obvious. While he found it embarrassing (because he didn't feel the same way about them), Warnie found it highly amusing to watch his younger brother politely trying to fend off unwanted romantic advances.

It wasn't that Jack was not attracted to women because he was; it was more that his mind was so active and intelligent that it would have been an unusual woman indeed that could have attracted him intellectually, and for Jack that was essential. We have to remember that Jack was an unusual young man, and so he needed to meet an unusual lady. He did in the end, but that comes later in the story.

Jack was a busy man in these days. He was running a household and catering to the whims and tyrannies of Mrs. Moore, who was slowly growing older and more difficult and made even the simplest job into a major production. He was trying to help raise a teenage girl while he himself was not much older than she was. He was just beginning a career as a writer and another as a university teacher, and he was also finding the truth of Christianity and its importance to his own life. For any woman to attract his romantic love, she would have had to equal his energy and determination in all of these areas. In fact, it might be honestly said that he simply did not have time for romance in his life.

Many of Jack's friends from Oxford often came to visit the family home at The Kilns, and they always found

Mrs. Moore to be a charming and hospitable hostess. Of course they never lived there and never saw her making her endless demands on Jack's time. She always went out of her way to let him spend time with his friends whenever they visited, but they all seemed to like her, and she made them feel that she liked them. Many people have this sort of Jekyll and Hyde ability and can be charming and entertaining with visitors or strangers and then revert to being beastly as soon as they are alone with their families. It is often a symptom of what we now call depression. The visitors temporarily distract the sick mind from its own inward pain, and the person will, for the brief time of their visit, be happy and lighthearted, charming, and cheerful; but as soon as the visitors leave, all the old pain comes flooding back, and they turn horrid again.

Warnie came home from his second posting to China, retired from the army, and took up full-time residence at The Kilns as a member of the family. He was able to help Jack with his chores and with the beginnings of something that was to turn into one of his most difficult and demanding tasks, his letter writing. Jack had already begun to write books that were to be remembered for a long time. Between 1930 and 1940, he published *The Pilgrim's Regress*, a book about his own journey back from darkness into the light of Christianity; *The Allegory of Love*, about medieval literary tradition; *Out of the Silent Planet*, which was the first of his three science fiction books; *Rehabilitations and Other Essays*, a book about literature; and *The Personal Heresy*, another book about literature. One of the results of all this publication was that Jack began to be known outside of his own immediate circle of friends and colleagues, and while this seems to be something that everybody wants to have happen to them, it turns out when you have got it, to be more trouble than it is worth. Jack began to get letters from people asking him things about his books. At first just a few, and Jack was pleased and flattered that people took the trouble to write to him. In those days, of course, letter writing was something that people did a lot more than they do today. Telephones and telephone calls were not as popular as they are today, and there were no fax machines or Internet for E-mail, so if you wanted to get in touch with someone, you either had to go to their home or write them a letter. Transport wasn't as good as it is today; there were no motorways, and fewer people had cars, so letters were the usual way for people to communicate with each other.

Jack began to get letters. Warnie was well able to help Jack with answering mail, as he had learned to type and had bought a typewriter. Of course this meant that Jack and Warnie had to work in separate rooms because Jack found the tapping of the typewriter keys very distracting, to say nothing of Warnie's occasional grunt or mild expression of annoyance when he hit a wrong key, which he did often. So soon, Jack would work at college or at a desk in his bedroom, and Warnie would tap away at his typewriter in his study, which was one of two rooms they had built onto The Kilns especially for his use. Sometimes he would work in one of Jack's two sitting rooms at college. Warnie began to write an occasional letter for Jack, to answer the easy questions, and just to help out a bit. Warnie was never a good typist. He always typed with just two fingers, and he made lots of mistakes, but at least everyone could read whatever he wrote. Jack, on the other hand, scribbled away with his dip pen, and over the years his handwriting slowly got worse and worse. Many people found his letters hard to read. Sometimes they even wrote back asking what he had said in his first letter!

Warnie began to fit himself into what he, with his many years of strict army routine behind him, thought of as the chaos of life at The Kilns. He began to get used to it,

though he never really liked the lack of any regular meal-
times and found the constantly reoccurring mini-crises
hard to take. Warnie just kept out of the squabbles of the
womenfolk as best he could and tried to keep his temper.
He drove here and there on his motorbike and ran the
errands he was asked with good grace but never too much
enthusiasm. Army life had taught him not to appear too
keen to do things because if you were too enthusiastic you
soon found yourself being asked to do more and more. He
knew that if he seemed too keen to help, he would soon be
spending all his free moments, and many that were not
free as well, running all over the place to satisfy the whims
of Mrs. Moore and Maureen, and he had no intention of
letting that happen to him as it had to Jack.

The Kilns outside and to outsiders became more and
more lovely while inside the family was learning how to
live with one another in comparative security. It's a funny
thing, but when people are stressed by having danger or
difficulty thrust upon them, they often find it much easier
to get along. It's probably because they are too busy worrying about the difficulties or dangers that are facing them
to have time to get annoyed or worried about the silly
little things that cause squabbles among families who are
in relatively easy circumstances. In any case, now that
Jack and his family were safely settled into their own
home and no longer had the fear of having to move hanging over their heads, and now that Jack had a good job
that could well (and did) lead to a successful career,
Mrs. Moore and Maureen began to find all sorts of reasons
for petty fights and foolishness. Jack tried not to get
involved in these any more than he could possibly avoid,
and Warnie also tried to stay out of them. Nevertheless,
there were always little disasters and fights between the
women of the household; little things that would not have
mattered in the least in the tough years began to seem

important. Jack managed to bear all of this with amazing patience and remained for the most part good-tempered and always ready to help in any way that he could. Jack had found a helper in the Holy Spirit of God, and he set about the tough task of putting his newfound Christianity to work in his everyday life, which is where it matters most. Warnie too was able to accept what he felt he could not change (though never quite as well as Jack) because he too had found Christ, and he tried valiantly to put his faith into action, and that is really the measure of a man.

Nothing lasts forever, and this time of relative peace and quiet at The Kilns was, like all other times, passing. Outside the quiet and peace of Oxford and The Kilns, major events and changes were taking place. Outside of England itself, across the sea in Europe, politics and economics were beginning to look dark and clouded with forebodings of trouble to come. As dark and evil clouds gathered in the minds of men, countries began to prepare once again, after such a short time, for that which all men should learn to hate and fear, war.

Chapter Nine

ONCE MORE INTO

DARKNESS

To understand what life was like for Jack in those days leading up to 1939, we have to look at what the other grown-up members of the family who lived at The Kilns thought about it. Warnie had moved into The Kilns with delight and high hopes that it would become a lovely and happy home for them all, but slowly over the years he began to be disappointed and dismayed. At first things went along nicely, but slowly and surely Mrs. Moore became more and more demanding of Jack's (and to a lesser degree of Warnie's) time. Warnie and Jack had both become Christians and were trying to live their lives based on love for God and for their fellowmen (both male and female). Now by that I don't mean love in the sense of some kind of manufactured emotion, some kind of "warm fuzzy" feeling, but love in the sense of action—what they did, not what they felt. It is interesting that what you do and what you say soon start to affect what you think and what you feel, and Warnie soon came to realize that Mrs. Moore seemed to have decided to live her life based on the opposite of love.

Mrs. Moore had certainly had a tough life. Her marriage had been miserable, and she had fled from a husband whom she always referred to as "The Beast," taking her two children with her. She had then centered her life on her son Paddy and her daughter Maureen. Paddy had been killed in the war, and she was badly hurt and bitterly angered by that, which seemed so unfair. Indeed it was and always is unfair for men to take actions that steal away other people's children by bringing them to an early grave. Mrs. Moore began to be both bitter and angry toward God and toward mankind. Slowly she fed on this bitterness and anger until it turned into hatred and rage, and she took it out on Jack, Maureen, and to a lesser degree on Warnie. Maureen, her own daughter, was growing away from her and began to argue with her all the time. That too simply fed her anger.

Slowly Mrs. Moore began to treat Jack more and more badly until it became obvious to Warnie that she regarded him as little better than a servant. Jack put up with this extraordinarily well, but then he had committed himself to taking care of her and of Maureen as long as necessary, and in his strong Christian faith he simply accepted whatever that might mean. He must have been tempted again and again to turn his back on her and all her tantrums and just stay at college all the time, but he didn't. Instead, he put his faith to work in his private life as much as in his public life, and that, what we do in our private lives, is a major part of Christianity.

Warnie had made no commitment to anybody in his whole life and found it hard to understand Jack's behavior. Slowly Warnie began to be uneasy with the way his brother was being treated and then to be annoyed by it and finally absolutely outraged. Having started out loving

The Kilns for its beauty and comfort, it was through these years to come that he grew to hate, loathe, and detest every stone, brick, and blade of grass of the place. It wasn't actually the place that he hated, but being a Christian, he would not allow himself to hate Mrs. Moore, so he hated The Kilns instead.

By 1939, Warnie was already becoming disturbed by life at The Kilns, but where Jack had college to escape to, Warnie too had his own escape. In 1936, he had organized a twenty-foot motorboat, called the *Bosphorus*, to be built to his own designs, and he would take off for days on end of what he called "ditch crawling," by which he meant cruising through the rivers and canals of England. He felt that there was no better way of getting away from the tyranny of life under the rule of Mrs. Moore than by simply taking a few supplies and going aboard his boat. I have to say that I fully agree with him. He would slowly putter along the river into the countryside and then cruise from pub to pub. Often he slept on board the *Bosphorus*, but sometimes, when he wanted a bit more luxury, he would tie up at one of the riverside inns and stay a night or two. England had relied for many years on rivers and canals for most of its transport, and there was then and still is today a network of waterways all over the country. Often Warnie would take a couple of friends along with him, and off they would go. In many ways Warnie reminds me of the Water Rat in *The Wind in the Willows*.

Jack was seldom able to get away for even a day because to do so would be to make Mrs. Moore unhappy, and she would take it out on everyone else in the household, something Jack could not allow. Things at The Kilns were getting steadily worse. Meanwhile, all across Europe, the same sort of thing was happening on an international scale. A bitter and angry man had come into political power in Germany, and he soon raised a large, well-equipped army and began to take over the countries around Germany one by one. In England everyone began to worry. Finally, only twenty-two years after the war that was so horrible that people called it "the war to end war," England could no longer stand by and watch as Hitler's armies invaded nation after nation, and England declared war on Germany.

At once life at The Kilns changed dramatically. Warnie was recalled to active service with the army and was sent off to France yet again. He was soon promoted to the rank of major (he was known as Major Lewis or "The Major" for the rest of his life), and although he was ill several times in France, he spent six months in action in what he always called "The Phoney War," in which little actual fighting took place. This was just the lull before the storm though, and in the end, when the fighting started in earnest, the British Expeditionary Force, as it was called, was driven back before the German army. Along with thousands of others, Warnie was evacuated with his unit from the beaches of Dunkirk in the most successful mass rescue of soldiers under fire ever to be attempted. He was soon sent home to Oxford as a reserve officer and volunteered to serve as a private soldier with the home guard.

Unfit for active service through his wounds in the first war, Jack was also determined to do as much as he could for his country in this desperate time, and he was soon lecturing for the Royal Air Force on Christian matters. It seems that what he said raised the spirits and morale of the pilots and airmen whom he addressed because he began to become a popular lecturer at RAF stations around the country and was asked to make several broadcasts on the BBC.

Meanwhile, however, life at The Kilns took on a different nature than that which it had enjoyed (or endured, depending on your viewpoint) before the war started. First, this war was to be different from the last one. This is something generals never seem to be able to learn, that a new war is always totally different from the one that preceded it. In the First World War two things had been invented which were to change the whole face of wartime life for the people living at home. One was airplanes that could fight; as well as transport bombers and fighters. The other was submarines. Bombers now allowed the vileness of war to be brought from the battlefields right into the cities and homes of the civilian populations of the warring nations. Submarines had been used to sink warships, but in this new war they were being used to sink merchant ships in an effort to starve the people of Britain into surrender.

So the first thing that had to be done was to protect the children of the cities from the danger of being blown to bits by bombs dropped from the sky. In England, children from London and other cities were evacuated to country areas, and soon several schoolgirls were living at The Kilns. Paxford and Jack had built and buried a concrete air-raid shelter up by the lake (it's still there; and if you walk from the house up to the lake, turn left, and work your way through the overgrown bushes, you will find it), and the house had to be fitted with black-out curtains so that at night no slightest gleam of light could escape the windows to attract the interest of enemy pilots. These were heavy curtains often made out of thick wool blankets of the same kind as were issued to soldiers or sailors in the armed forces. Air raid protection (ARP) wardens were appointed to walk around on patrol at night, and the cry of, "Oi! Number 27, dowse that glim!" and the like were often to be heard as the warden spotted a gleam of light from the windows of number 27 of whatever street he was patrolling at the time. At The Kilns, at first the blackout was achieved by a whole conglomeration of towels, rags, spare clothes, blankets, and all sorts of weird and wonderful bits and pieces, but eventually, heavy navy blue and khaki (of the English olive green sort) blankets were tailored to fit the windows, and only the last chinks were filled with odds and ends of material to seal in the light. They also helped to keep the cold out, and this was important because all the coal, which was the main fuel burned in the fireplaces and boilers for heating, was soon to be needed for running the steam engines of ships and trains. Coal for household use became hard to get.

The family car was sold because it was soon apparent that no one was going to be able to get petrol, which was also needed for the battle tanks, trucks, and planes for the war, and thus family outings came to a stop. Slowly, rationing was introduced, and it became more and more difficult to feed the family. Mrs. Moore's chickens soon became a valuable asset, as did Paxford's shotgun, which deterred people from stealing the eggs (and indeed the chickens themselves). Fred never actually shot anyone, but he shot close to a few people before the word got around that it was not a good idea to try to lift an egg or two from The Kilns chicken coop and indeed could be hazardous to your health. The coal ration was subject to theft too. It was kept in the old kilns themselves, and they were soon fitted with locked wooden gates, and Fred had to instigate a nightly patrol of the grounds. Being a thoroughly honest man himself, Fred tended to become disgusted and annoyed at the dishonesty of others. For the most part though, the people of England began to pull together to face the dangers of Nazi Germany.

At The Kilns life became different and in some ways much tougher though in other ways much better as well. The girls staying in the house were mostly nice enough, and some of them were absolutely wonderful people. One who stood out during those years was a young lady named Jill Flewett. Mrs. Moore was growing more and more crotchety, and she criticized and abused everyone available from dawn to dark. Jill Flewett simply took all of this in stride and never lost her patience. She worked unceasingly at all the menial tasks to which Mrs. Moore put her, and Jack and Warnie soon grew to love her as if she were their own daughter. For some reason they nicknamed her "June" and even after she had married and become Mrs. (later Lady) Clement Freud, she remained a friend to both Jack and Warnie for the rest of their lives. Years later Jack was to model his character Lucy Pevensie after her.

Jack was desperately worried in the first few months about Warnie, who at the age of forty-five was away in France with the British Expeditionary Force. Jack never knew whether Warnie was under fire or safely under cover somewhere, and he was in an agony of worry in May 1940, when the British Expeditionary Force was beaten back through France to find itself stranded on the beaches at Dunkirk. Warnie was among the thousands of troops taken off the beaches by almost any craft that could float and make way under its own power. Warships; merchant ships; coastal tramp steamers; civilian ferry-boats, fishing boats, and pleasure craft, large and small— all answered the call to rescue the soldiers from Dunkirk. Under constant attack from the air and from artillery, they pulled in as close to the shore as they dared and loaded up with as many soldiers as they could carry. Many years later I was on a lobster fishing boat in South Wales and asked about a row of equally spaced and neatly patched holes in the side of the cabin. "Aye," said the skipper, "machine gun, got them from a Messerschmitt at Dunkirk." All sorts of little boats trundled their way across the English Channel and brought home almost all the troops. Warnie was soon back in England and, much to Jack's relief, was transferred to the reserve list and sent home.

∞

Jack was doing all he could to make life at The Kilns at least tolerable for those who had the misfortune to be unable to escape from Mrs. Moore's rule, and Warnie too joined in this effort. Jack and Warnie both joined the home guard and found themselves patrolling through the night the back streets of Oxford, rifle in hand. Jack was traveling around England from RAF station to RAF station and delivering lectures about Christianity to men who knew all too well that they would probably die in the near future. It was work that he found both tiring, partly because of the endless traveling in overcrowded trains, and emotionally draining. He also made broadcast talks on the radio with the British Broadcasting Corporation.

England slowed down and dug in. Cities were blasted from the skies by wave after wave of Nazi bombers, and young men went off to fight. It always seems unfair that wars are made and planned by the middle aged and elderly but have to be fought by the young. Jack watched in horror the bright young men going off (as he himself had done not so long ago) to kill and to be killed. There really isn't any way to describe how absolutely ghastly life at The Kilns was during those years nor, I suppose, any real need to. Jack stuck to his commitment to look after Mrs. Moore and kept his temper as she grew more shrill and illogical. Her brother had suddenly gone totally mad some years before, and now she herself was losing touch with reality and with any ability to recognize what was true and what was not. At the same time she was able in these years to put on a good performance for Jack's friends whenever they came to visit, which was not often as they too had their war work to do.

As the war went on, the news was almost always bad for the first few years; and as things seemed dark and

getting darker, depression and despair seemed to invade
The Kilns. Tempers grew short, and the days were filled with
arguments about nothing, back-biting, lies, and petty
squabbles. To Jack it was slowly becoming an unpleasant
place to live. To Warnie it was almost unbearable. There
were bright spots in the long, drab, drawn-out days of senseless little jobs and meaningless fights. June was one, and
friends at college were others. The Inklings particularly were
a source of great joy and comfort to Jack and Warnie both,
and now they were meeting regularly every Tuesday and
Thursday. A new face had arrived in Oxford with the Oxford
University Press (OUP) transferring its offices and staff to
Oxford to get them out of London, and a writer whose
works Jack had recently read and had admired moved there
with the OUP. Charles Williams was now based in Oxford.

Jack and C. W., as he was often called, were soon firm
friends, and Warnie and the others liked him too. He was
a valuable addition to the Inklings, for he had a lively
mind and a fund of knowledge about all the things that
interested them.

Jack had already begun to have many admirers in
America, and this was a fortunate thing for his family and
for the Inklings because, as the war progressed, German
submarines began to sink so many ships on their way to
England with important goods and materials that almost
everything started to get scarce. England even in those days
was already relying heavily on imported goods and even
foods, and with most of the young men away fighting all
over the world, there was a real problem with raising
enough food for everybody to eat. Young girls began to
sign on to what was called the land army and began driv-
ing tractors and doing the farmwork that had always been
done by men in the past, but food of all kinds was already
scarce. Luckily, Jack's friends and admirers over in America
soon learned how bad things were in England and started

to send him parcels of all kinds of food and other things that were impossible to obtain in England. Anything that arrived addressed to Jack at The Kilns was shared with the family and the girls staying there, and anything that was addressed to him at Magdalen College went into special feasts for the Inklings. Sometimes clothes were sent over, even several dinner jackets or tuxedos. The dinner suits didn't fit Jack, to whom they were addressed, so they were handed on to those who could wear them. One was raffled, and the man who won it, Colin Hardie, was the wrong size too, so it went to Christopher Tolkien whom it fit very well, and for all I know he may have it still.

Jack was grateful for the generosity of his American friends, most of whom he had never met, and he never forgot their kindness. Their gifts made a long and lean time more bearable for him, his family, and his friends. It is notable though that Jack didn't hoard or sell any of his American presents but shared them equally with friends and family. Sometimes he even sent them on unopened to someone he knew of who was in poor circumstances and in more need than he himself.

One of the best ways to get through a tough time is to work as hard as you can, and this is what Jack, and almost everybody else in England at that time, did. Warnie, much to his delight, found that being the owner/skipper of a motorboat got him the job of river patrol, and the government supplied him with petrol to cruise up and down the rivers and canals every so often, making sure that all was well and that no windows facing the water were showing any light. So really he was doing what he loved most and doing it officially to help the war effort and being paid for it as well.

Jack worked as hard as he had ever worked in his life, if not even harder. He traveled and lectured, and wrote and broadcast until he was utterly exhausted.

Life at The Kilns went busily on with the changes mak-ing things little more difficult in fact, but Mrs. Moore behaved as if the entire war was designed merely to make her life more miserable. One of the chief differences was that every evening before any lights were turned on, the heavy blackout curtains, in two layers, had to be carefully drawn across the windows. This job was one which Jack and Warnie always did when they were home and Paxford did when they were away. Warnie liked to draw the cur-tains while it was still daylight because he said that if he could see daylight coming in, then anyone outside after dark would be able to see light coming out. Also there was always the problem of apportioning the right number of ration coupons out so that when Paxford went to the shops he made sure that he had the right coupons to buy whatever was the family's allowance of the available food. Paxford also learned how to repair shoes and boots because new ones were impossible to get, and old ones had to be made to last. The cobblers were mostly away fighting, so Paxford was the one to whom this task fell. If it had not been for Paxford, with his many talents and his undefeatable cheerfulness while all the time saying the most uncheerful things, the family would have been far worse off than they were. Paxford himself was working at a factory beating out steel panels for tank bodies and fit-ting them together, but in every spare minute he had from his factory work, he was constantly thinking of and doing things to make life easier and better at The Kilns.

Maureen was by this time a grown-up lady. She had been teaching music at Headington School since 1935 and still living at The Kilns, and she too did her best to make things easier for Jack. In 1940 she married Leonard Blake, also a music teacher, and moved away. The house-hold was sad to see her go, but of course everyone wished her the best happiness.

The only way Jack could be so kind and patient with an old lady who was steadily losing her mind was by his determined effort to put his Christianity into practice, not just now and then but every minute of every day. If nothing else, his life at The Kilns at this time was excellent practice for being Christian. It became an opportunity to test himself and everything he believed in, to see if his faith worked if he did Christianity instead of just talking about it, and to see if he was man enough for the job. Jack found that Christianity really does work if you try hard enough and never give in for a single moment to spite, anger, or dislike. He also found much to his own surprise that he was man enough to put up with all the niggles and nastiness, and it wasn't till much later looking back at it that he actually realized how bad things had really been.

The war dragged on and on, and although most of England was a hive of activity with bombers and fighters in the skies above, for most of the time Oxford and The Kilns were little havens of comparative peace. Once or twice the air-raid sirens sounded, and the family would quickly walk up to the air-raid shelter and wait inside until the all clear was sounded. Once, late at night, a German bomber, probably lost and heading for home, unloaded its bombs on top of Shotover Hill where they probably scared the dickens out of the rabbits, foxes, and badgers who lived up there. The war for the most part did not impact too hard on Oxford itself, but of course the people suffered as much as anyone else. Jack saw a great deal of the horror of this war as he had of the last one, for he traveled around from city to city and from RAF base to RAF base. He saw the shattered remains of what had been beautiful cathedrals and towns. He saw the hollow eyes of the young fighter pilots who took off every day in their Spitfires and Hurricanes to combat the Germans invading their skies, and he saw too the wounded brought home to try to heal, bodies, minds, and spirits devastated by man's incalculable inhumanity to man. On his trips he learned that the desperate conditions everywhere else made the difficulties he suffered at home seem to be unimportant and not worth getting upset about. This was a valuable lesson for Jack and one we should all try to learn. When things looked their worst and an invasion seemed about to happen, Jack suddenly remembered that his old First World War officer's pistol, a Webley Scott .38 revolver, was still in a drawer in his bedroom. He thought that if the Germans did invade, anyone whom they found in possession of a weapon would be immediately executed along with his entire family. And although he felt inclined to keep it and fight as best he could, he did not think that his personal pride was a good enough reason to put his household at risk. Early one morning, before dawn, he put the pistol in his pocket and walked to Oxford. He paused on Magdalen Bridge, and taking out the pistol, he hurled it as far as he could into the river. Somewhere at the bottom, deep in the mud where all such implements should be put, it is probably still there.

Chapter Ten

MOVING ON

Eventually, after years of hardship and tragedy, the war came to an end, and England had to try to gather together its tattered remains and put things back onto a normal footing. The shortages that had begun during the war were even worse after almost seven years of fighting, and rationing continued well into the 1950s. Jack, now forty-seven years old, had worked heroically throughout the war years and was completely drained of all energy by the beginning of 1946. Plagued with headaches, suffering from nightmares, and always feeling desperately tired, he was often ill, sometimes seriously. Every flu virus or infection that went around the neighborhood seemed to attack him, and he had not the physical strength to resist them. Living as he had for long years on a poor diet and constantly over-worked, he was not only tired but also very weak.

In 1940 Jack had published a book called *The Problem of Pain*, and it looked at the age-old question of why God allows us to suffer. It was a classic book and is still available today. Pain was something that Jack was beginning to understand fairly well, and his book took a long and careful look at it. Jack had the unusual ability to study what was happening all around him and indeed within him and then to write a careful account of it in a form that was easy to read and useful to other people. Being almost continually under temptation as all Christians are, the best Christians more than anybody, Jack had the idea of writing a book from the point of view of someone doing the tempting. Then he took it even further and wrote a book of letters from a senior and experienced demon to his young nephew who was just starting his career as a tempter. This was called *The Screwtape Letters*. These letters first came out in serial form in a newspaper, and later, in 1940, in a book. Jack also wrote a book all about Milton's great poem *Paradise Lost*, which he had first read when he was nine years old. This he called *A Preface to Paradise Lost*, and it was published in 1941. His talks for the BBC were also written up and published as a book called, naturally enough, *Broadcast Talks*, and that came out in 1942. And the second volume of them was released under the title *Christian Behaviour* in 1943. Jack also wrote his second science fiction book, *Perelandra*, at this time, and it too was published in 1943. He wrote a book about the teaching of English in schools that was released in 1943, called *The Abolition of Man*. In 1944 another new book came from his pen, *Beyond Personality*, the third volume of his BBC talks. In 1945 the third book in his science fiction series, *That Hideous Strength*, was released. In 1946 a sort of dream fantasy about heaven and hell came out called *The Great Divorce*. In 1947 he wrote a book called *Miracles*. In 1948 he wrote two books: *The Arthurian Torso* about his friend Charles Williams's work and a book of essays called *Transposition*.

Throughout his life, Jack was being occasionally visited by ideas, or not exactly ideas so much as pictures in his head. When he was about sixteen, he had a sudden picture of a faun carrying an umbrella in a snowy wood.

There is no record of it, but I bet it made him smile. Later on, when he was about forty, he thought that he would like to make a story out of it, but it was not until around 1949 that anything began to come of the idea.

At about this time, around 1946, Jack came to the conclusion that he himself was not very important. By that I mean that his physical body was not important, and his own comfort was less so. For this reason he was far more likely to worry about and take care of other people than he was to take care of himself. He may well have been right in one sense in that it is far more important that we concern ourselves with other people's welfare than with our own. If everybody did, then everybody would be taking care of everybody else, and we would not have to worry about ourselves at all. Jack, though, saw this as something to be practiced rather than just as an idea, and so he set out to do it. He fussed and fretted over Mrs. Moore, Warnie, and the girls who were staying at The Kilns during the war, his friends, and even people whom he just happened to meet, but he never fussed over himself. What he did not realize was that this habit was to have fairly dire consequences later on and lead to his causing other people a great deal of anguish which could have been avoided or at least delayed for some years. Jack soldiered on, shouldering his work at college and his work at The Kilns, and he took care of everyone around him as much as he was able.

Warnie was by now becoming more and more of a problem to Jack. Warnie saw the problem that Mrs. Moore had become, and he hated it; but just the same, he too was loading Jack down with almost constant worry. Warnie was an alcoholic, plain and simple. He finally began to admit to himself that he had a problem, but he was never able to face up to it and do anything concrete about addressing it. He tried hard and with some success to stay sober, but when things got tough at The Kilns, he began to turn more and more to drinking to try and escape from his difficulties. When Warnie was sober, he was one of the finest gentlemen you could ever meet, and in these times he was sober for months and sometimes even a year or more at a time; but when he began to drink, he just wouldn't be able to stop until he was unconscious. Warnie was a man with a constitution like an ox, and that meant he would drink huge quantities of alcohol before finally passing out and would be in considerable danger of alcohol poisoning.

When he was at home in Oxford, he was often able to stay completely off the drink, but if he went away for a holiday or any kind of trip, he soon succumbed to temptation. He never had to face the difficulties of life by himself and for himself, and now in his late forties he discovered to his horror that he was simply unable to do so. Sometime in about 1947, Warnie had to sell his boat, the *Bosphorus,* and he began to feel more than ever that he was trapped at The Kilns. He let this feeling weigh heavily upon him, unlike Jack who simply accepted life as it was and did his best within it.

Jack had little opportunity for any kind of holiday and tended simply to live from day to day, working as hard as he was able from early in the morning to late at night. Mrs. Moore made his life thoroughly unpleasant all day every day. Warnie was completely at a loss to understand why he put up with it, and some of Jack's friends of the Inklings also found it difficult to understand. They privately asked Warnie why Jack accepted this life, but Jack would not discuss it with Warnie, and Warnie was unable even to guess at the reason. I believe that it was simply that Jack had become the sort of hero who having decided to undertake a task just would not give up on it until it was finished, no matter how difficult or unpleasant it became.

In 1947 Maureen persuaded her mother that Jack simply must have a break, and she came to The Kilns to take
care of the old lady while Jack and Warnie went to
Malvern. Maureen now lived there with her husband
Leonard Blake, who was by this time music master at
Malvern College, Jack and Warnie's old school. Jack and
Warnie both man-aged to have ten days of freedom and
relaxation walking the Malvern Hills and spending time
together. Warnie did the cooking and Jack the washing up.
Also in 1947, while on holiday in Ireland, Warnie first
drank himself into a hospital in Drogheda, a town that was
to become a regular place for his recovery from alcohol
poisoning for years afterward. It is significant of how badly
this terrible disease of alcoholism had attacked him that he
also began at this time to lie to himself and others about
it. He even lied about his drinking in his own diaries.

Jack worried about him and did not have any idea
how he could help his elder brother. He began to try to
keep alcohol away from Inklings meetings and out of their
home. It didn't do much good though because Warnie
could not understand that Jack's reluctance to open a bottle of wine was actually for his sake and not anything to
do with Jack's preferences. Uncharitably he put it down
to Jack's stinginess, but he was lying to himself, for he
knew that Jack was by nature the most generous of souls.
Alcoholism was poorly understood then, and it was considered a disgraceful personal weakness rather than a disease, as it is thought of today. The truth about it is
probably somewhere in between these two ideas and perhaps a bit of both. In any case, Warnie's alcoholism was
considered to be an utter disgrace to him and to his
family, and so it was kept as much of a secret as possible.
Looking back on it now, it is probable that this secrecy did
more harm than almost anything else could have done to
Warnie's health. Secrets are always dangerous and evil

things and in this case particularly so. In those days it was
only good manners to offer someone an alcoholic drink
almost whenever you met them, and all the Inklings
would have been in the habit of inviting or even encouraging Warnie to drink. After all, they didn't know that he
was an alcoholic. That was a secret. If they had known,
they probably would have been able to help him quite a
lot simply by never tempting him. The destructive nature
of secrets was not understood back then any more than
was alcoholism.

Life was made even more difficult and unpleasant by
the fact that in 1947 even potatoes were put under
rationing. Thus without potatoes to fill up on, for the first
time in their lives, Jack and Warnie (and everybody else)
had to go to bed hungry every night and get up hungry
every morning and never be able to eat enough to feel full.
They were hungry all the time. Paxford did his best to help
by growing as many vegetables, including potatoes, as he
could in the garden at The Kilns. Fred worked hard to con-
tribute as much as possible to the family, but throughout
the war and immediately after it, he too was working long
hours at the steel panel factory where he made parts for
tanks and did not have much time left to work at home.
Jack would deliberately eat less than his share so that
others might have more. This too did not improve his
health. Jack never complained and never lost his temper
though at times he held on to it by sheer force of his own
willpower; he was very much practicing his Christian faith.

The brightest part of this time for Jack and for Warnie
too was the twice-weekly Inklings meetings. They were
encouragement and friendship, professional criticism and
discussion, and good times. It is probable that only these
meetings of good friends made life bearable for Jack. His
virtual slavery at The Kilns, his worries about Mrs. Moore's
fast declining mental and physical health, and his worries

about Warnie would all be pushed to the back of his mind by the good talks and fellowship of rich and powerful minds.

Finally, in 1949, Jack's health gave out almost completely, and he collapsed. Very ill indeed, he was taken to the hospital in an ambulance and received penicillin injections every three hours. However, his stay in the hospital of a week or so did him more good than anything had in years. Nobody could get at him, and he was forced to rest, as visitors were restricted to only a short time each day. Humphrey Havard explained to Warnie that Jack's main problem had been caused by being run down by overwork, and Warnie, in a fine fury, accosted Mrs. Moore, insisting that she allow Jack to go for a month's holiday. If it had happened, it would have been (according to Warnie) Jack's first real holiday in fifteen years. However, for some reason or other, perhaps because Warnie went off to Ireland by himself and promptly drank himself into a stupor, Jack stayed at home at The Kilns and went back to work.

Sometime around this period Jack began to have a series of nightmares about lions, one lion in particular, not just a big lion, but a lion with a distinct personality. And slowly his mental pictures of the faun with his parcels and the lion began to come together in his mind. He started to work on a book that was to change the world. It grew gradually at first but soon took off and flowed from his pen. In this book much of what Jack loved about life all came together. It had landscapes from his beloved Ireland, and trees, waters, and woods from The Kilns. It had characters and creatures from ancient mythology and from the fields and hedgerows of the countryside of both Ireland and England. There was great good and desperate evil such as Jack had found here in the world in which he lived. There was treachery and heroism, the things of which all great tales are made. This new book was something the like of which Jack had never written before, and come to think of it, nor had anyone else. It was not a sensible, clever, and wise book for grown-ups; it was a sensible, clever, and wise book for children (though grown-ups should read it too if they want).

He read passages and chapters of it to the Inklings, and everyone except J. R. R. Tolkien met it with great enthusiasm. Tolkien was a mythical purist who did not like the way in which Jack had deliberately mixed mythologies in the book, despite the fact that all Jack's mythological creatures and personalities stay true to their mythic origins and characteristics throughout the book. Tolkien was a narrow-minded man in some ways, and he felt that mythology, which was his passion, should be kept separate and pure. He was not as widely read as Jack though and probably failed to realize that Jack knew a great deal more about the mythology of the world than he did. In any case, Jack was not discouraged and forged ahead to write what has become one of the best-selling children's book of the twentieth century, if not of all time, *The Lion, the Witch and the Wardrobe*.

∞

This book, *The Lion, the Witch and the Wardrobe*, was the first to be written (though not the first of the series) of the seven Chronicles of Narnia, and is an exceptionally valuable book. I believe that in writing it, Jack was influenced by the Holy Spirit of God because within a completely fictional fairy tale it manages to give a guide to its readers of how to understand what God did for us in this world by coming here and sacrificing Himself for us.

Jack was already a famous writer and teacher by 1949 when he was writing *The Lion, the Witch and the Wardrobe*, and he was already getting letters from all over the world, but neither he nor anyone else could have guessed how much this was to be magnified by the publication of this apparently simple book. It is interesting to note that while Tolkien was desperately discouraged by people continually rejecting his *Lord of the Rings*, it was Jack who encouraged him again and again to keep writing and to keep sending the book to publishers until at last a publisher called Unwin accepted it. Tolkien, on the other hand, tried to persuade Jack not to send *The Lion, the Witch and the Wardrobe* to any publisher because, he said, people would laugh at Jack if it were to be released to the public. Jack encouraged Tollers, but Tollers tried to **dis**courage Jack. In the end, of course, it turned out that Jack was right about both books. *The Lord of the Rings* has become the greatest work of fantasy for adults of the last century (some people say of the last millennium), and *The Lion, the Witch and the Wardrobe* and the rest of the Narnian Chronicles have become the greatest children's fiction.

In 1950, just as things seemed to be at their worst, they began, as they often do, to get better. First, Mrs. Moore's elderly and spoiled dog that she insisted should be taken out for walks over and over again (it was easier and less bother simply to do it than to argue about it) finally up and died, and no one was sorry to see him go. At last one of the foolish and annoying tasks was lifted from Jack's tired shoulders.

Then a few months later Mrs. Moore herself was considered by her doctor to be too old and sick to be cared for at home any longer, and she was moved into a nursing home called Restholme. Now Warnie, who by this time really found it hard not to hate Mrs. Moore, also found it difficult not to rejoice that she was taken away out of the house, to be looked after by professional nurses and people instead of Jack. But he knew that it is evil to rejoice over other people's misfortunes, and he tried hard to keep his emotions under strict control. Jack went to visit her every day, still fulfilling that same promise that he had made some thirty-two years before to Paddy Moore. But at last, at long last, The Kilns was filled with peace, and quiet reigned throughout the house.

Warnie at first could hardly believe she was gone and spent his time always tensed waiting to hear her shrill cry calling to Jack to come and do some idiotic and unnecessary chore, but finally the fact of her absence began to sink into his mind. He could see that Jack was slowly unwinding too, and bit by bit the apprehension and nervousness began to seep away. Jack was able to work solidly and uninterrupted for hours at a time, and both brothers were able to establish a routine in their lives. Instead of meals being ready at any time at all, so that you never knew how much time you had to work or to get something done, they were able to instruct their housekeeper that lunch should be served at one o'clock every single day. They actually knew what time lunch would be. It may sound like a small thing, but to two scholars and writers it was important for them to be able to organize their time. Then again, tea would be at four o'clock, and dinner at seven every day of the week. You always knew where you were in the day and when you had to lay down your pen and go to the dining room.

Jack had said for years that he didn't like "fancy foods" but just good plain cooking. This was true but not for the reason that people think. He did not actually prefer simple foods to more complicated cooking; it was just that Mrs. Moore, who had been in charge of the cooking for

years, would always make a major performance of anything in the least out of the ordinary. Jack simply preferred
to have her attempt only the simplest of dishes. Of course
when he dined in college, he enjoyed the fine food and
wines very much but was careful not to develop a taste for
things he knew would lead him to resent the plain fare he
would always get at home.

The cooks and housekeepers they could afford to
employ were not well trained (if trained at all), and so
they simply ate what the cooks could prepare. In later
years Jack and Warnie were to enjoy cooking of the
highest standards, but that was a while ahead yet.

Something else happened in 1950, which seemed at
the time nothing of any great importance. Jack received a
letter from a Mrs. Joy Gresham from upstate New York. As
was his principle, he answered her letter, and a correspon-
dence soon grew up between them. From the very first, her
letters stood out from among the hundreds he received.
They were well written, amusing, and intelligent, and both
he and Warnie were impressed by them and by the mind
behind them.Mrs. Gresham had written to him because
she had been making her own journey of discovery. She
had traveled from childish atheism, being a starry-eyed
member of the Communist party, to slowly having to
admit (much as Jack had years earlier) that God was there
and that He was in charge, finally coming to know Jesus
personally as God Himself who came here in the flesh of a
man and is here today as the Holy Spirit. Part of this discovery was helped by her reading Jack's books, and she had
some questions, so she wrote to him. Mrs. Gresham herself
was a writer, and she appreciated good work.

Jack was now as near to being a happy man as he
could be. *The Lion, the Witch and the Wardrobe* was published in October 1950 and was met with enthusiasm
by all and sundry. In the same month a year later, he

published the sequel called *Prince Caspian.* He was able to plunge into his work now that there were no tiresome distractions at home, and his duty was reduced to visiting Mrs. Moore once a day at Restholme. Then in January 1951, she died, and Jack was freed of even that duty. It is hardly surprising that Jack's writing changed a little in character at this time. In 1952 he revised his earlier short books of broadcast talks and combined them into one book called *Mere Christianity* and also released the third Narnia book, *The Voyage of the Dawn Treader.* A year later, in 1953, *The Silver Chair* came out. Jack was now becoming a famous man. His mail increased by leaps and bounds, and soon a lot of his time, and a lot of Warnie's time too, was spent simply writing letters.

Jack's pen friendship with Mrs. Gresham, or Joy as she was called, also had grown and developed. And in 1952she came to England and asked if she could meet him and Warnie.

Chapter Eleven

AGAPE, PHILIA, STORGE,

AND *EROS*

Being the extraordinary man that he was, Jack had never found himself in love. This was partly because he was so gifted intellectually that he never met a woman who could keep up with his lightning-fast thinking nor one who was interested in the same things that he was to the extent that he was. It was probably also at least partly because he had voluntarily accepted a responsibility for Mrs. Moore, Maureen, and Warnie that left him little time or emotional energy to spend on anyone else. Third, it was also partly because Jack took a different view on love from that which most people hold. Perhaps I should explain that a bit.

Jack believed that one of the failings of the English language is the fact that we have only one word for love. The ancient Greeks used four. *Agape* was their word for the love of God, which flows through one person to another. This is also called "charity," and it should be the basis of any relationship between people. Then there is their word for the love of friendship, and that is *philia*. This is the sort of love that one has for a dear friend that makes you like to be with them and spend time doing things together. Third is what the Greeks called *storge*. *Storge* is the sort of love that you feel for someone who has been a part of your life for a long time, and if they go away, you miss them far more than you ever thought you would. They leave a hole in your emotional life that no one else can fill. Fourth is the love that girls and boys start to be affected by when they grow-up; the Greeks called it *eros*, and it is also called "romance." Now in today's world people are always rabitting on about "falling in love," and all they mean is a romantic attraction. Romance doesn't last and soon passes away, and if that is all that two people have to base their relationship on, they are in trouble. Jack was determined that the right way to form a relationship was to start with *agape*, wait a while to then see if *philia* develops, then wait some more to find out if *storge* is becoming a part of what is happening, and then finally to wait for *eros* to show up. If all of these things happened, Jack would have considered that he was "in love." To him it had just never happened. He had studied this matter and even written a book about it, *The Four Loves*.

Jack had read the great love poems and love stories, but he had no firsthand experience of what they were talking about. He had watched some of his close friends "fall in love," get married, and then spend years wondering why on earth they ever did. His whole world, and the way he looked at it, was all to change, and Jack was to pass from a sort of half-satisfied contentment into the roller coaster of love and happiness shot through with great pain and sorrow at the same time.

In 1952 Jack's pen friend, Mrs. Joy Gresham, the Christian writer from America, came to England. She wrote to Jack asking if they could meet, and she and a friend of hers came to Oxford to meet Jack, having invited him to lunch at the Eastgate Hotel. He was so impressed by her that he returned their invitation and asked them to lunch with him at Magdalen College, which, after all, was only good manners.

Joy too was an extraordinary lady. Her parents were Jewish, but neither of them had any faith in God; and they brought up their two children, Joy and her younger brother Howard, to be atheists. Joy made the long and difficult journey to Christianity later in her life. From her early childhood, Joy's father, Joseph Davidman, realized that his daughter was no ordinary child. He was a high school principal in New York, and he brought home IQ tests to try to find out how intelligent his children were. Howard had a high IQ, but when Joseph tried the test on Joy, her scores went off the scale. She had excelled in her schools and at college and was widely read. She was also gifted with a total-recall memory, or at least with the facility for it, which she deliberately developed just as Jack him-self had done. By the time she and Jack met, she was already a poet and novelist of some small reputation and was working on a book called *Smoke on the Mountain*, which was all about the Ten Commandments (first published in 1953, it is still in print today, fifty years later). She was thirty-seven when they first met, and he was almost fifty-four.

Jack had probably been a bit nervous when he went to meet this stranger in Oxford. One is always a bit apprehensive when actually going to meet someone whom one has written to. However, Jack soon found that he was facing a mind as sharp as his own and a wit every bit as quick. What's more, he discovered that here was someone as widely read as he was and in some areas even more so. Not only had she read everything that he had and more, but she also remembered as well as he did and understood nearly as well as he did. For Jack to meet anyone as bright and as educated as himself was unusual, if indeed it had ever happened at all, which I doubt. He had certainly never met a woman who fell into this category. Jack was delighted, and a friendship soon grew between them. Jack read her book in manuscript and liked it enough to agree to write a foreword to it, and for a writer as well-known as Jack was to do this would ensure that the book was taken seriously. Joy stayed in England for several months. She had left her cousin Renee (who had fled from a bad marriage and a dangerously violent husband, and was staying with the family for safety at our home in upstate New York) as a sort of housekeeper to take care of her husband, Bill, and her two sons, David, then about eight, and Douglas (me), six and a half. However, after many merry meetings and after earning the friendship and admiration of both Jack and Warnie, she returned to America.

Jack and Warnie continued their settled routine life, and time ticked past at a slow and sleepy pace. Then in 1953, Joy returned to England. Her marriage was in ruins, and she brought her two sons with her. It was her wish to escape from all that her life had meant to her in the past and to start again in England. Joy loved England, and at that time it was a cheaper place to live than America. Her husband, Bill, had "fallen in love" with her cousin Renee; and after he and Joy were divorced, he married Renee and became a fine husband and stepfather to her two children (right up until he died at his own hand after being diagnosed with cancer in 1962). Joy settled in London and began to try to earn a living for herself and her two sons.

Jack had long been in the habit of giving away two-thirds of his income from his books (despite the fact that he was always poor and feared poverty), and this charity fund was used to pay school fees for the two young American boys at an English boarding school. Joy and the boys lived in London for about two years and then moved to Headington. Joy had found that her friends, those whom she liked most, were all people to whom Jack and Warnie had introduced her, and she wanted to be where she could enjoy the good company and conversation they found customary. Jack and Warnie were two of her best friends, and when she and the boys moved into 10 Old High Street in Headington, Jack and Warnie were two of the most frequent visitors there.

Jack had suffered all his life from the difficulty of finding others with whom he could converse an equal. In many cases he was regarded as decidedly odd because of his strong and public Christianity. Those men at Oxford who resented his success were often the same men who resented his Christianity. Time and again he was passed over for election to a professorship, the positions often going to less able and less qualified men. Meanwhile, over in Cambridge this was not going unnoticed, and in 1954 Cambridge University offered Jack what is known as the "chair" (that means professorship) of Medieval and Renaissance English Literature. This was a new chair at Cambridge and was created to fill a need and with Jack in mind for the job. When the authorities wrote to Jack, offering it to him, he at first said that his responsibilities in Oxford made it impossible for him to accept. Now think about this; here was Jack being offered the very job for which he had longed for many years, the one job that suited him best in the world, and to which he was the best-suited man, and he was saying no. It might seem hard to understand until we remember what sort of man we are talking about. Jack was a man who had learned to put his Christian duty before any other consideration, and he felt that his responsibility to Warnie and to Paxford outweighed his own personal wishes, ambitions, or comfort. Warnie was thoroughly settled in Oxford and at The Kilns. Now that Mrs. Moore was gone out of his life, Warnie was happier than he had ever been before, and only his occasional lapses into alcoholism cast a shadow on his contented and comfortable life. Paxford too had become completely settled into life at The Kilns, and he too was a happy and contented man. Incidentally, he had become a good cook, in that sort of studied English fashion of boring food, and often provided the meals for Jack and Warnie. For Jack suddenly to move to Cambridge would mean that Warnie and Paxford would lose their homes and Paxford his job as well, and Jack simply felt that it was his duty to protect them both. Jack regretfully wrote and explained that he felt he could not accept and explained why.

The electors at Cambridge were not so easy to dissuade though, and after a series of letters back and forth, they made Jack understand that they would be happy for him to live and work at Cambridge during the week in term time, and return to his Oxford home on weekends and during vacations. Under these terms Jack was happy to accept the new job, and he was given a suite of rooms at Magdalene College Cambridge. So Jack moved from Magdalen (Oxford) to Magdalene (Cambridge, both of them pronounced "Maudlin").

Joy had also had the problem of being isolated on the pinnacle of her own intellectual ability, never meeting anyone with whom she could converse at the same level as her own lightning-fast mind was used to working. Even the Inklings could not quite equal Jack, and in Joy for the first time he had met his match, and in him she had met hers.

A sort of example of how these two minds worked was to watch them playing Scrabble with each other. It was their favorite game, but to make it more interesting, they used one board, but the letters from two Scrabble sets, and then allowed words from all known languages, factual or fictional. As long as the word really existed in some book somewhere and they could prove it, they could use it.

There were those among the Oxford set that surrounded Jack who found this brash and superbly knowledgeable New Yorker hard to take, mainly because she did not expect to have to be gentle with those who posed as great minds, and she pulled no verbal punches. It was a time and a place in which women were not expected to be the equal of men in intellectual pursuits, and even if they were, it was considered ill mannered for them to show it so blatantly. Joy was not only the equal to the men she met but in most cases their superior in many fields of knowledge, and some of them resented the fact. The really good men with good minds welcomed her though and gleefully crossed swords with her in discussion and debate. Joy attended occasional Inklings meetings and more than held her own in the good-humored verbal sparring that was the hallmark of these occasions. Warnie found her to be a delightful companion as did Jack.

Her home, 10 Old High Street, Headington, soon became a meeting place for some wonderful people. I loved the place. It was a small house, but it had a garden in the back where Joy grew vegetables, and there were fruit trees too. More important to me was the fact that The Kilns with its woods and lake was only a short walk away (though when I was little, it seemed quite a long way for me), and I was welcome to play in the gardens and the woods.

In 1956 someone in the British Home Office decided that Mrs. Gresham's visitor's visa was not going to be renewed and that she would have to take her two boys and go back to America. This was a terrible blow to Joy. She loved England and had established a new life in that country. She had a circle of friends around her whom she loved, and she loved the different way of life that she had now grown accustomed to. Also, she felt that English education was far better than American and dreaded uprooting her two sons yet again and taking them back to America. She needed advice and turned to her best friend, Jack, to seek it.

Jack could only think of one way of preventing her deportation back to America, and so he offered to undergo a civil marriage ceremony with her to extend to her the legal formality of his British citizenship. Neither of them regarded a civil marriage as of any validity in the eyes of God, and they would both continue to live as they had before, she in her house and he in his, but legally they would be married. Joy and her sons would have the right to remain in England under Jack's extended citizenship. I think also that Jack was reluctant to lose a good friend, one in whom he had found an equal mind. In any case they were duly "married" in a registry office in Oxford on Monday, April 23, 1956. Warnie was not aware of this "marriage" till much later, as he was not sober at the time when Jack decided on it, and only Jack's closest confidants were told. Those whom Jack consulted about it were Arthur Greeves, his oldest friend; George Sayer, who had been a pupil and had become a friend; and Roger Lancelyn-Green, another old pupil and friend of both Jack and Joy.

∞

Jack and Joy continued to live as before, he at The Kilns, where she often visited him and Warnie, and she at 10 Old High Street, where Warnie and Jack often visited her. Things might have gone on like this for a long time if something quite sudden and shocking had not occurred.

Joy was suffering from pain in her hip, and it was getting steadily worse. Finally, her leg just gave out on her and broke. She was taken to the hospital where it was discovered that she had a severe case of cancer. The doctors soon determined that she was dying and had only a few weeks or, at the very best, a few months to live. Jack found to his surprise that he was heartbroken at the thought of losing this true friend whom he had found only such a short time ago. The two boys were at school, but when the term ended, they went to The Kilns to live with Jack and Warnie while Joy was in the hospital.

The doctors did all that they could for Joy, but by March 1957 they had given up all hope. Warnie described the day that he heard that she was dying as "one of the most painful days of my life." It should have been a happy day, for on that day, Thursday, March 21, 1957, Jack and Joy were properly married by an old pupil of Jack's, a good and true friend, Peter Bide, who had become a priest of the Anglican Church. It was not a traditional wedding. There were only Jack and Joy, Peter Bide, Warnie, and Joy's nurse at her bedside in the Wingfield Hospital in Oxford; and Joy was expected to die within a few days. Immediately after the ceremony Peter Bide laid his hands on Joy and prayed to God that He should heal her if it be His will. I too had prayed hard to Jesus that He would do something to give my mother back to me because she was the only person I really knew in the whole world.

Joy was sent back to The Kilns to die in peace in her husband's home, but she didn't. She got better instead. God was so good to both Jack and Joy. He snatched Joy back from the jaws of death and gave them to each other so that they could spend a few years together in the kind of happiness that neither of them had ever experienced before.

Some interesting things happened to Jack and to Joy at this time. One was on an occasion that Joy was suffering from extreme pain in her legs. Jack prayed to God that if it was allowed, he should be permitted to take over the pain until an injection of strong painkiller, which had been administered by the nurse, could have time to work. At once he felt an indescribable agony settle into his legs, and Joy sighed with relief. The pain in Jack's legs lasted until Joy's injection took hold, and then it eased away. Also, Joy's bones began to regrow. Her body was finding extra calcium from somewhere while, at the same time, Jack found himself suffering spasms of agonizing pain in his back. The doctors found that he had a condition known as osteoporosis, which is a loss of calcium from the bones, making them soft and spongy. So while Joy was gaining calcium from somewhere, Jack was losing his.

Steadily and at first slowly, Mrs. Joy Lewis began to recover. Soon she was judged to be out of danger. The doctors could not understand what was happening and regarded it as a miracle. She was supposed to have died within a few days of coming home, but instead the cancer was receding, and her health was steadily improving. By December 1957 she could walk again, and at once she set about bringing some order and comfort back into The Kilns. The house now had both electricity and a telephone, but since Jack and the family had moved in, in 1930, no redecorating or repair work had been done to The Kilns at all, and it was in a bad state. Joy also managed to get Paxford enthusiastic about the vegetable garden and the flower beds again; they too had been sadly neglected over the years since the war. The greenhouse was rebuilt and a new heating system installed in it. The central heating system in the house that had not worked in years was overhauled and put back into working order. Soon the house was a bright, warm, and comfortable home.

Now while this amazing recovery (of The Kilns as well as of Mother) was taking place, something else equally amazing and even more beautiful was also happening. These two people, one in her forties, and the other in his sixties, fell in love in the proper, really and truly sense. They had met as Christian brother and sister, and the love of God, the *agape* had flowed between them. Then they had discovered their like-mindedness and the fact that they shared so many interests and characteristics, and *philia* grew up between them to hold them together as fast friends. Then when it seemed that death was to part them, they both became aware that they most feared losing each other. *Storge* had joined *agape* and *philia*, and then finally, after they were married both legally and before God, *eros* arrived to complete the quartet. These two, who already had a firm base of three kinds of love to build on, built one of the loveliest of love stories on the ashes of forlorn hopes.

When Joy was well enough, they began to go out on trips into the countryside together. Jack had long known and loved Studley Priory, an old Elizabethan priory which had been converted to a sort of academics' club and then later to a hotel. He would hire a car with a driver and would often take Joy there for Sunday lunches and afternoon teas. They explored the countryside around Oxford driven by the same private hired car with their regular driver Clifford Morris. As Joy got better and better, she joined Jack and Warnie as they started once again with renewed enthusiasm to bring the woods back into some sort of shape. For many years the local young people had made the woods at The

Kilns a sort of public park that they invaded all the time and vandalized as they wished. Joy decided to put a stop to this and had a barbed-wire fence built. The wire was cut, and she bought a shotgun. Trespassing soon stopped, and the woods and the lake became once again a place of peace and quiet where you might expect at any minute to see a faun pop out from behind a tree.

Jack was absolutely in love with Joy, and she with him. They were as happy as two people could ever have been, but they were not living in any kind of fool's paradise. They both knew that Joy's good health was not going to last for long. They knew that God had given them a time of glorious love and learning before Joy would have to go on to be with Him. They both knew it, and yet they did not let it spoil their enjoyment of each other and the limited time they would have together. They went on trips together, one to Greece, which they had both always longed to see, the home of the great myths and legends, and to Ireland so that Joy could see the landscapes that were the basis of Narnia. They went on holiday to Wales together, and Joy helped Jack to write a book that he thought was the best he had ever written, called *Till We Have Faces* (now, many years later the rest of the world is finally beginning to agree with Jack that it is his best book).

If you could go back in your time machine and listen to the two of them talking, you would be struck at once by two things that stood out whenever they were together. One was how much fun they always had in each other's company, and the second was how very much they loved each other.

Warnie had been a bit nervous at first about Joy's moving into The Kilns, and after the years of Mrs. Moore, it is not at all surprising. And he wondered if he should move out. Jack and Joy made it very plain that they wanted him to stay living at The Kilns and be a part of the family just as he always had, and taking him aside, Joy had said quietly to him, "It may not be for very long, you know." Warnie decided to give it a try and stayed. Soon he grew to be glad that he had. All his life Warnie had longed for a sister, and in Joy he finally found one. Jack and Joy had met a lady named Jean out at Studley Priory, and she became Joy's best friend. Jean was a motoring journalist and was always being lent new cars to try out and write about, so during the term time when Jack spent his weeks at Cambridge, Jean would come over to The Kilns, collect Joy, and the two would take off on some crazy adventure trip through the wilds of the English countryside. This was back when England still had a few real wilds left. They would tour around half lost half of the time and loving every minute of it. Then when Jack came back for the weekend, Joy would tell him hilarious tales of their adventures, and they would laugh together. Jean and Warnie were the two people who protected Joy from loneliness during the long weeks when Jack had to be away in Cambridge. Jack was also learning how to be a good stepfather during these hard, happy years that they spent together, and Warnie was doing his best to learn how to be a good stepuncle, if there is such a thing.

Jack was happy to be able to invite his friends to come and visit at The Kilns. In the years before Joy had the place renovated, his friends had called The Kilns "The Midden," an old English word meaning a rubbish heap, and few had cared to visit the place, and fewer still had dared to eat there. It wasn't actually as bad as they made out, but in my first years there, I fell through the floor of my bedroom which was rotted out with fungus; and on another occasion the ceiling fell down just missing me as I leaped for the door, warned by some instinctive message possibly sent by an angel. Now visitors to The Kilns found a fresh, well-decorated home filled with warmth and love, and even better they found good food well presented, placed on the dinner table. Joy was a brilliant cook, and she had patiently taught the housekeeper and even Paxford how to make the best use of the foods and to present a real feast at every dinner-time. She crocheted a beautiful lace tablecloth for the dining table too. Guests at The Kilns became more frequent and were welcomed not only by the inhabitants but also by the house itself, which now seemed proud to show itself off to strangers.

By this time Jack was an internationally famous writer and teacher, and his mail was a major task each day. When Warnie was home and sober, he undertook to answer many letters on Jack's behalf, tapping away with two fingers at his old typewriter; and when he was away, Joy took over the job. She also typed out all Jack's writing while she was well enough.

It couldn't last forever, and it almost seems unfair that it lasted so short a time, but we (like Jack and Joy) must remember that the few short years they had together were, in themselves, a gift from God and thus something to be grateful for. In October 1959 the cancer came back, and Joy began again her long fight against the disease. Apart from her great warmth and humor and her amazing intellect, one of the things that everyone who knew her well always remembers about Joy is her astonishing courage. She met her illness with her head high and fought it to the last.

One thing she had always wanted to do was to visit Greece, the land from which all her favorite myths had come, and she and Jack were able to do just that. In April 1960 Roger Lancelyn-Green and his wife June arranged for Jack and Joy to accompany them on an eleven-day tour of Greece. Very ill, in almost constant pain, and often in a wheelchair, Joy traveled around in the bright doom-laden sunshine of that ancient land, she and Jack reveling in this wonderful adventure. Joy was dying, and she knew it. Jack knew it too, and both of them knew that the other knew, and yet they were ecstatic as they journeyed from place to place, seeing for themselves the ruins of the great cities of Greek mythology. They arrived back at The Kilns desperately tired, and both very unwell, but happy and resigned to whatever the Lord allowed to come next.

Two and a half months later, on Wednesday, July 13, 1960, Joy died. The sensation of emptiness that filled The Kilns when she was gone was so strong that it almost felt solid. People say, "Prepare yourself," when something like this is coming. Well you can't. It doesn't matter how long you have known that it is coming or that it must happen sooner or later; you just can't be ready for it. It still feels like being hit on the head with a hammer. Jack had known for almost four years, the happiest four years of his life, that this moment had to come, the moment when returning from the funeral and entering The Kilns, he would find it empty, but the reality was staggering, and his grief was absolutely overpowering.

He did what he always did when under extreme stress. He sat down at his desk, and looking into himself and carefully observing what was happening deep in his mind where we keep our inmost secrets, he picked up his pen and an old exercise book and began to write.

Chapter Twelve

HOME AT LAST

J ack triumphed over many difficulties throughout his life. He had defeated the terrible experiences that he had suffered at the hands of foolish (and in one case insane) teachers at schools. He had come wounded but victorious off the battlefields of the First World War. He had passed through the trap of self-reliant atheism to find his way to Christ. He had defeated the difficulties of poverty, long and aching responsibility, overwork, illness, and exhaustion and had found in the end love and happiness, Joy and joy. Now he faced perhaps the greatest challenge of his entire life, the loss of the woman he had loved so much for so short a time.

Jack's grief was hardly describable, and yet he tried to do just that. He sat at his desk and wrote down what he was feeling, the pains and the temptations, the deep grinding emotions that worked their way through him all arrived on the paper beneath his pen. He not only wrote this journal, but he read it back to himself as he wrote it day by day. In doing so, he discovered a great deal about the nature of grief and what it does to us. Although he was not writing for publication, his friend Roger Lancelyn-Green came to visit a few

weeks later, and hearing from Jack what he had done with
his journal, he bravely asked if he might read it. When he
had done so, he realized at once that this journal had the
potential to help thousands of people, for all of us at some
stage of our lives have to face the fact that we are not here
forever, and sooner or later someone we love will go on
ahead of us, leaving us behind.

Roger urged Jack to publish this account of his grief.
Jack was reluctant to do so because in those days such a
personal baring of the emotions would be regarded as
embarrassing to both Jack himself and, more importantly
to him, to his friends. He was persuaded, however, and he
tidied it up and sent it to his literary agent with instruc-
tions that it should be published by a publisher with
whom he had never published before and under a pen
name to hide his true identity. The agent sent the book to
Faber and Faber under the pen name of Dimidius (which
means cut in half), and they at once decided that they certainly wanted to publish it, but on the board of Faber at
that time was T. S. Eliot, the poet. Now Eliot had become
a friend of Jack's despite the fact that Jack couldn't stand
Eliot's poetry and had not been slow to say so. Eliot was
sure that he recognized who had written the piece and
suggested that he use a less distinctive pen name. So the
book soon came out as *A Grief Observed*, under the pen
name N. W. Clerk (Anglo-Saxon: "Nat Wilk Clerk," meaning no one knows the writer). It wasn't until after Jack
himself had died that it appeared under his own name.

Jack was half the man he had been, and in one sense
he was never completely happy again. He settled back to
work and to continue his life with an aching emptiness
that nothing could ever fill. His love had left him to strug-
gle on alone, and yet not alone because in his darkest
time, when all else had gone, he found in the empty

stillness that the Holy Spirit of God was with him and still loving and caring for him.

The Inklings meetings continued, though they took a while to get going again and never really recovered from Jack's move to Cambridge, his marriage, and his loss, for he was the focus of them. In a formal sense the meetings had ceased around 1949 or in the early 1950s, but the group of friends still met from time to time, if perhaps less formally than before. There was still much merriment and laughter, but somehow for Jack at least, it was never quite the same.

Jack also had a new responsibility to take care of, two teenage stepsons, each presenting the typical problems associated with growing up, though each in his own unique way. As was typical of the man he had become, Jack did everything he could to help these two young men. He knew all too well from his own life's experiences how difficult their lives had been and tried hard to do the best he could for them.

For a while life at The Kilns settled down again and slid into yet another new pattern. Warnie, who had loved Joy as much as Jack had, though in a different way, found her loss hard to take; and he turned to alcohol to try, unsuccessfully, to ease his pain. In late 1960 Jack himself was exhausted after years of constantly caring for someone as sick as Joy had been and Warnie was, and living in that strange mixture of joy, happiness, fear, and sorrow. His long years of caring for Mrs. Moore stood him in good stead, for the years of constantly caring for someone who really wasn't sick but pretended to be had almost been training for the task of looking after someone who genuinely was dying. But Jack's habit of regarding everyone as more important than himself had taken its toll on him and his own health. He was by this time a sick man. Nobody who did not know him well indeed would ever

have guessed it though because he didn't complain.
Indeed he made light of his own illness and joked about
it. He wrote a book entitled *An Experiment in Criticism* and
another book, a series of fictional letters to a fictional
character he called Malcolm, this one about prayer. It was
called *Letters to Malcolm*. Before Joy's death he had been
working with her on a new novel, which he had planned
to call *Menelaos Yellow Hair*. It was the story of the ancient
Greek king Menelaos and his rescue of his wife Helen after
the defeat of Troy and their adventures on their voyage
home. But after the loss of his own Helen, he had not the
heart to continue with it. I have always regretted this
because he gave me the manuscript to read and read parts
to me, and I thought it was going to be a wonderful book.

Jack went back to Cambridge and continued with his
work, but his trips home to The Kilns on weekends were
no longer met with Joy but with a house inhabited but for
him strangely empty. Warnie began to be drunk more
often and was of little assistance for much of the time. The
two boys, when they were home, were more of a liability
and responsibility than anything else. There was little to
come home to that Jack could really look forward to. But
then there was the peace and the sense of Joy's presence
occasionally with him, and he was content to wait upon
the will of God.

Jack had needed an operation for quite some time. He
had not been taking care of himself at all while Joy was
slowly dying and had worked himself to a shadow in taking care of her. By 1961 he was in poor shape. So poor was
his physical condition that the doctors did not think he
was strong enough to withstand any surgical procedure,
and so he was in a kind of catch-22 situation. He needed
the operation in order to get well and strong again but
was not well or strong enough for the doctors to risk the

operation. Jack had an inflamed prostate, and it needed to be removed, but it had resulted in an infection that damaged his kidneys, and this put strain on his heart.

In the latter part of 1961, Jack was forbidden to use the stairs at The Kilns, and so he slept in what had been the common room or the sitting room of the house and worked in Warnie's study, which was on the ground floor. He still continued to work almost as if it was simply by habit. He had been left with a weak spine by the loss of calcium from his bones and had to wear a back brace at all times. He slowly had to accept that he was and always would be an invalid, but he was careful not to let it show any more than was completely unavoidable. His condition improved again for a while, and in 1962 he was back at Cambridge, still writing and teaching.

Jack had realized by late in 1961 that he was coming to the end of his eventful and productive life. He wasn't an old man, but he felt like an old man. However, it is important to realize that Jack was ready to go on and be with Jesus. He did not long for death but was ready just to wait and accept whatever the Lord sent. Jack had defeated every move that Satan had sent against him through the power of the Holy Spirit of God, and he had no illusions as to the source of his victories. Now, once again loaded with responsibilities—two orphaned teenage boys, an elderly alcoholic brother, and a household—bereaved and sorrowing, ill and tired, Jack discovered one of the greatest secrets of life: that no matter what is actually happening around you, you can still be content if you hand your life over entirely to Christ. Jack settled into a contentment that is hard to understand. He had to retire from Cambridge University. He was no longer able to go for the long walks he had delighted in. He was not allowed to drink wine or beer, not allowed to eat anything other than a strict diet prescribed by his doctors. All the pleasures of his life had been taken away from him as also had been the love of his life, and yet he was content. He was in that rare state in which his physical disabilities and his emotional distresses no longer affected his happiness or lack of it. He had finally become able to make God the center of his life and to regard himself as merely a bit player in the drama. He was not exactly happy; he had merely come to the conclusion that his happiness was not what he should be seeking at all. In fact it was completely irrelevant, and therefore he was content to be without it.

Jack suffered a heart attack brought on by his weakened condition, which in turn was caused by his kidney infection, and he spent time in the hospital, not really expected to live. However the time was not yet, and he returned to life and laughter. At one stage the poisons from the infection running through his bloodstream caused him to suffer from hallucinations, and he said and did some strange things; but when he realized what had happened, he laughed about it. The only thing he had left was his mind, and that too at last seemed to be deserting him. Jack thought it a good joke and one more lesson to be learned that no matter what we are most proud of, it can vanish like a puff of steam on a hot day. He laughed delightedly at the fact that even now God was still teaching him things that he needed to know.

Jack made a point over the last few months of his life to invite as many of his friends as he could to visit him. He suspected that each time he said good-bye to one of them, it might well be for the last time. Jack had some help in the summer of 1963. A young American fan of his,

Walter Hooper, came over to meet Jack and stayed on in England for some weeks before he had to return to America. He frequently visited The Kilns and kindly made himself available to help Jack in any way that he could.

Jack put his affairs in order, did his best to provide for his brother and his stepsons, and answered his letters as he always had. Few of his friends had any idea as he gaily saw them off after a visit that he was dying and knew it. Warnie came home, and he took his turn in caring for his younger brother for those last months. He looked after Jack with great devotion, for Warnie too realized that Jack was going to go on ahead and leave him behind, just as Joy had already done.

On Friday, November 22, 1963, the famous writer Aldous Huxley died. On the same day in Dallas, Texas, John F. Kennedy, then president of the United States of America, was shot dead. Also on the same day at 5:34 in the afternoon, C. S. Lewis died at his much loved home, The Kilns, Kiln Lane, Headington Quarry, Oxford. He was the finest man I ever knew in my life, and I miss him to this day. But he was ready to go. He had done all he wanted to do and said all that he wanted to say; and more important still, God was ready to take him home.

Jack left behind him a large number of loving friends, a huge number of admiring acquaintances, and untold millions of fans around the world, and he also left a mass of unpublished manuscripts of things he had started and then rejected or started and not had time to finish. Walter Hooper, who volunteered to help by doing this difficult and laborious task, had cleared out his rooms at Cambridge. Jack had been in those rooms a relatively short time, but he was missed when he left. Those rooms and The Kilns contained the results of thirty-five years of almost constant writing, and the task of sorting through all of that too eventually fell to Walter Hooper. Now, some thirty and more years later, after Walter has dedicated his life to the task, almost everything Jack ever wrote has been collated and brought before the public.

I am sometimes asked what it is like living in the shadow of such a great man, and I always point out that Jack did not leave a shadow behind him but a glow. If I am able to reflect even the slightest spark of that glow, I am more than happy to do so. Jack left us Narnia, the wonderful land of Aslan and Tumnus, of the White Witch, of unicorns and dragons, high adventure and endless joy. He left us Glome, that dark and dreadful city; and in showing us the way out if it, he taught us how to lift our veils. Jack left us Malacandra and Perelandra and showed us the dangers and the joys that lie in wait for us in such places of the soul. And more than this, he faced the darkness that he found in this world and lit for us bright lamps to show us the path that all of us need to find. You will find them in the shelves of any good bookstore or library. Just look for the name C. S. Lewis.

Warnie lived on for another ten years after Jack's death, but the double blow of the loss of Joy followed quickly by the loss of Jack was really too much for him, and in his later years he turned more and more to alcohol. His loneliness and sorrow were such that he found himself unable to cope with life, and he died in 1973, a broken, sad, and lonely old man.

Maureen sold off The Kilns after Warnie died. She inherited it according to the agreement made back in 1930, and it passed into the hands of "developers" who promptly tore down the kilns and the barn, tore up the tennis court, tore out the orchards, and covered the whole area with houses. Even the front lawn has a house sitting on it, and The Kilns itself is now completely surrounded by them. The house is now owned by the C. S. Lewis Foundation of Redlands, California, and they have restored it back to the style and decor that it enjoyed back when we all lived there, and thus returned it to the style of the period in which it was designed. It is to become a residential center for serious scholars studying Jack, his works, and theology. The house itself actually looks better and is in better condition today than it has been since the 1960s.

The woods and the lake were donated to the Buckinghamshire, Berkshire, and Oxfordshire Naturalists Trust by Doctor Stephen, who bought it years ago. BBONT, as the organization is called, has tried to "manage" the area, and as a result it is less delightful than it was back when I lived there. To give them credit where it is due, they have tried to save the lake from silting up completely by pumping a lot of mud out of it. When they did so, they found Jack and Warnie's old punt at the bottom along with my old kayak. They only did about half as much as was needed though as they were short of money to spend on doing it properly, and you could not swim in it today as we used to years ago.

The air-raid shelter that Jack and Paxford built and in which I used to camp now and then was turned into a haven for bats, by bricking up the entrances, but when I was last there that too had been vandalized.

All the fields that once were around The Kilns are now covered with houses, and it is thus that beauty passes away. Enjoy, study, and treasure what you have around you now, for in time it will all pass away and change, and even if nothing else changes as you grow, everything you love will seem to shrink. The long weary miles you travel to school will soon be just a short hop (which is why grown-ups never understand how far anything is), and the world will shrink around you. The one place Jack loved which does not shrink is Narnia. Narnia just keeps getting bigger and better as we all go further up and further in.

—Douglas Gresham
Ireland May 1997, May 2000, August 2003